The Comple
Greenwich Park

Chris Hawkins

Copyright © 2021 Chris Hawkins. All rights reserved.

Unless otherwise stated, maps, illustrations and photographs are by the author.

Images marked CC are licenced under https://creativecommons.org/ and those marked PD are public domain (out of copyright)

Ormidea Publishing
www.myguidedwalk.com/ormidea

info@myguidedwalk.com

ISBN:	**978-1-739-9519-1-7**
First Published:	November 2021
First Edition:	November 2021
Edition / Revision	1 / 1 M

Contents

Introduction 2
Ecosystem 9
Before Enclosure 11
Humphrey, Duke of Gloucester 26
Henry VIII 32
Elizabeth I 40
James I and Queen Anne 43
Charles I and Henrietta Maria 46
The Commonwealth 47
Charles II 49
William and Mary 50
The Great Landscaping 54
The Park Wall 65
Greenwich Castle 77
The Royal Observatory 80
Views 105
Park Keeper 117
Park Ranger 120
The Queen's House 132
A Park for the People 137
Greenwich Fair 140
Attracting Visitors 147
Under the Park 153
The Park that Never Was 166
Trees 170
Historical Trees 199
Other Noteworthy Trees 206
Planted Areas 214
The Wilderness and Deer 224
Wildlife 230
Birds 232
Insects 234
2012 Olympics 236
Greenwich Park Time Line 238
Further Information: 247

Introduction

It might be surprising to learn that over forty percent of Greater London is open space and there are three thousand parks. Among these are the eight Royal Parks of which Greenwich Park is the oldest and most historic, having been enclosed in 1510 by Duke Humphrey, Protector of England during the reign of Henry VI.

Although it is one of the smaller Royal Parks by acreage, to the inquisitive visitor it appears much larger, as the eye is forever being disorientated by its undulating landscape, distracted by its outstanding views and enchanted by its remarkable buildings.

Providing a beautiful and inspiring green space for the residents of South East London, it is also a popular

destination for visitors wanting to escape central London for a day. Since 1997 Greenwich and Greenwich Park have been protected under international law as a UNESCO World Heritage site, an accreditation granted because of its importance to the world, both historically and aesthetically.

Greenwich and its park are inseparable, with one defining the other, and neither making sense on its own. Nothing typifies Greenwich or the park more than the iconic Royal Observatory standing proud at the top of the hill. Visible from the Thames and the London Docks, the bright red time ball still signals one o'clock every day as it drops back down to its resting position having slowly risen to the top of its mast a few minutes earlier.

From the observatory we can see all the way to the Docklands and City of London, the view stretching along the winding River Thames from the Shard at London Bridge to the O2 entertainment complex. Right before us lies the beauty and symmetry of the Queen's House and Old Royal Naval College, buildings that are integral to the story of the park.

Geology and Prehistory

Sixty five million years ago Greenwich Park was at the bottom of a large warm and shallow tropical sea. Gradually a thick layer of a soft limestone called chalk built up as small marine animals died and their shells slowly accumulated on the seabed.

Ten million years later, the area became coastal, with sand and pebble beds being laid on top of the chalk. As the sea deepened, silt from the eroding land masses settled on top of the pebble beds forming a deep impermeable layer of London Clay.

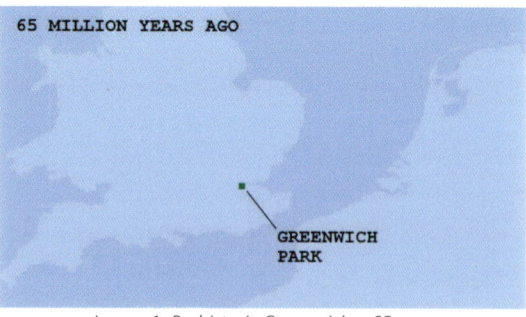

Image 1: Prehistoric Greenwich – 65mya.

Around fifteen million years ago the European Alps were pushed into the sky and the enormous pressures that caused them to rise thousands of meters above the sea also buckled and raised the whole of the South East of England. This created a huge dome of which now only the sides remain as the North and South Downs where the comparatively hard chalk was less fractured and resisted erosion.

Just beyond the North Downs, the London Basin formed, but even here the layers of rock and clay were lifted and distorted, in some cases breaking apart in violent earthquakes that shook the area and separated the layers, leaving faults. A line of these faults is responsible for a gravel escarpment in South East London which forms a natural barrier for the Thames. Greenwich Park, which is on the escarpment, is particularly heavily faulted, with the sand and gravel layers to the south being over 30 metres higher than they are to the north.

As the ancient seas receded, the land that makes up Greenwich Park emerged in a landscape very different to that of today. Trees became dominant and Greenwich Park would have been part of a huge forest. The River Thames had formed, but was flowing through present day Hertfordshire and was a tributary of the much larger Rhine. Britain was connected to Europe and the Thames joined the Rhine on land that is now below the North Sea.

The last ice age reached its peak just 22,000 years ago when glaciers had formed as far south as North London. These glaciers blocked the Thames and it adopted a new route where it was bounded by the glaciers and the escarpment of South East London, roughly its route today.

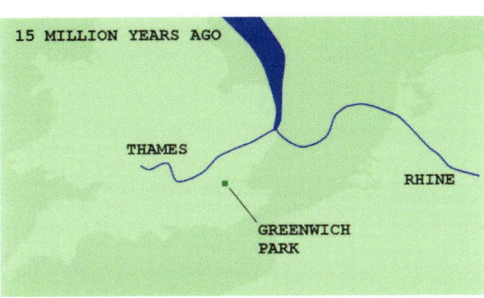
Image 2: Forests - 10 mya.

When the ice age ended, 10,000 years ago, the climate warmed quickly. The glacial melt water created a huge natural lake in the low lying land of the North Sea. This rapidly growing lake eventually breached the strip of land retaining it. Billions of tons of water burst out in a cataclysmic flood, gouging out the Straits of Dover and separating Britain from Europe.

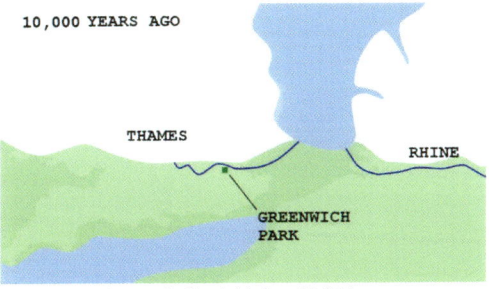
Image 3: Glacial Lake - 10,000 ya.

The Thames now had its own estuary into the North Sea, and over time it eroded much of the soft clay in London and laid down its own alluvial deposits.

The escarpment that runs along the south side of the Thames for several miles and makes up the hills and valleys of Greenwich Park, stopped the Thames moving any further south.

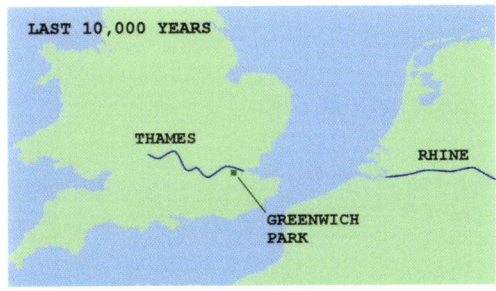
Image 4: last 10,000 years.

Relieved of the weight of the glaciers, Northern England began to slowly rise and Southern England began to sink. This process is still happening and each year London gets closer to sea level by about one millimetre. This fall in the land allowed the sea to flow back up the channel created by the Thames to make it a tidal river, where the water level rises and falls by around six meters twice every day. The Thames was not constrained by man-made walls as it is now and the tides meant that it had marshy and infertile floodplains either side which were bordered by temperate forests and heathland.

The meandering of the Thames around the Isle of Dogs at Greenwich, resulted in stronger and faster currents on its outside bank, causing more erosion. This pushed the southern bank of the river ever nearer to the high and dry ground of the escarpment.

The escarpment was solid, well drained and well away from the unhealthy marshes, but because it was so close to the river, it also provided ready access to the sea for fishing and a major route for trading. Above it the Blackheath Pebble Beds of the Harwich Formation formed an even more erosion resistant layer.

These characteristics encouraged Neolithic man to settle here around 6,000 years ago and begin to shape the landscape by creating farmland and coppicing the woods, a practice that would have continued until the park became primarily used for leisure.

During occasional flood events, the Thames would deposit material on its banks. The barrier of the escarpment at Greenwich forced these flood deposits upwards to create a small solid embankment on the southern side. This had helped make the location a good harbour for early settlers, and after some strengthening of

Meridian Line Geological Cross-section of Greenwich Park

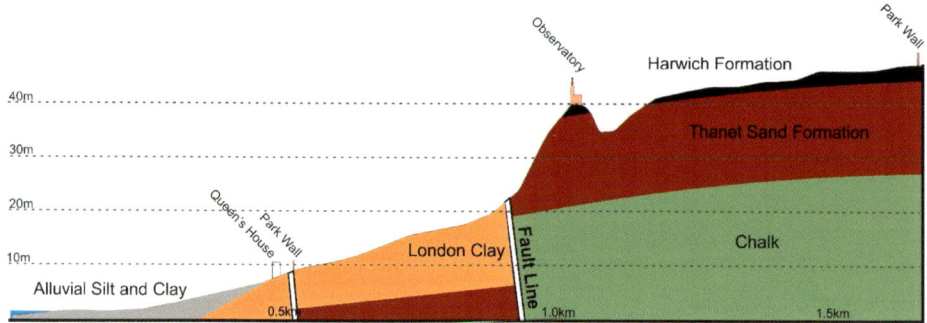

Image 5: Simplified Geological Cross-section of Greenwich Park along the meridian line

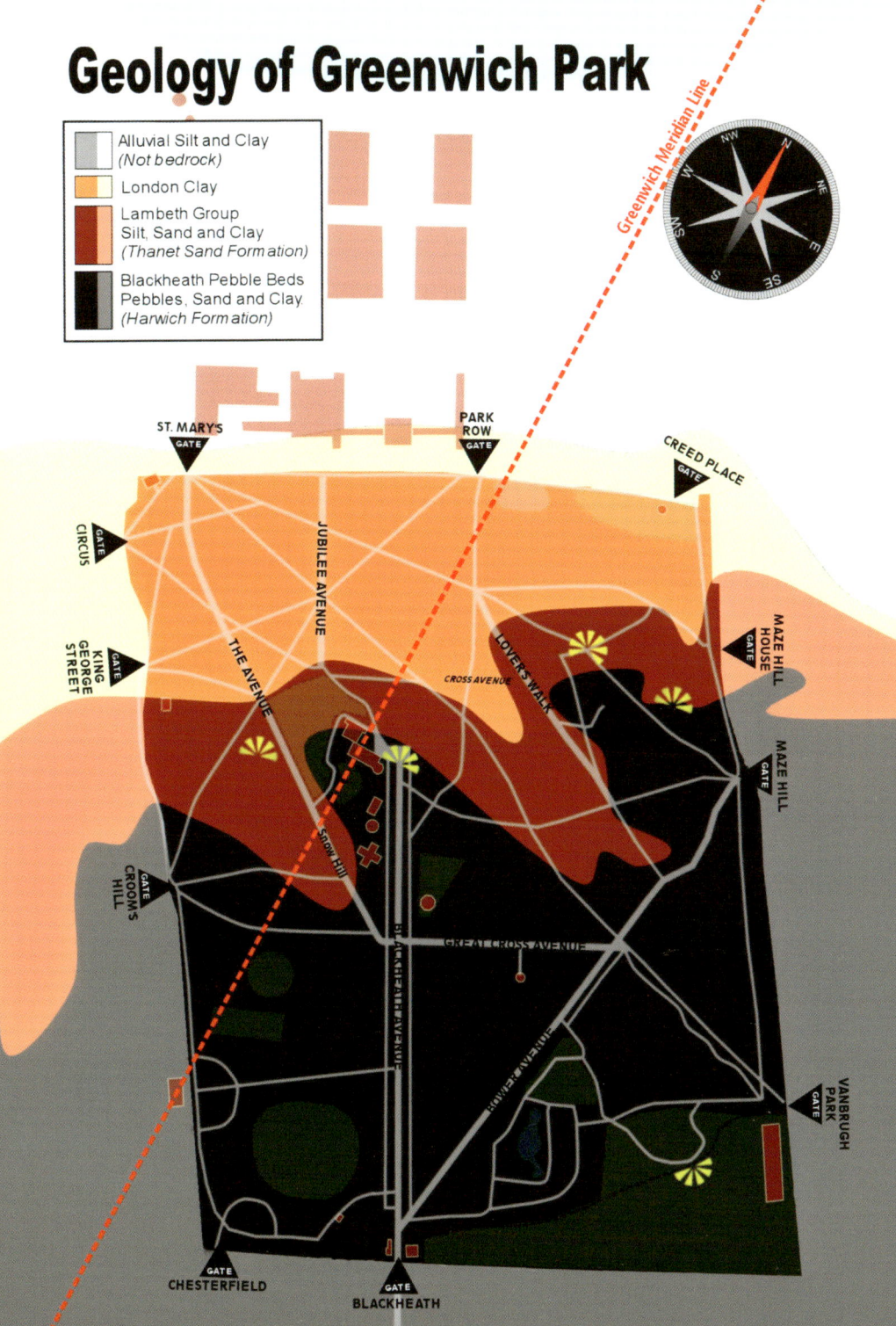

the river bank, it was high enough to avoid flooding and solid enough to build on. This facilitated the construction of the many great buildings that have fronted the river at Greenwich for the last thousand years or so.

The park is laid out across the escarpment from this slightly raised bank to the relative heights of Blackheath. The lower northern areas are clay, the escarpment itself is sand and gravel, and the upper southern areas are gravel where the poor soil results in a biologically diverse acid grassland landscape supporting many unusual species.

There are several places where this gravel and sand was quarried, leaving large hollows in the ground. In the park, these include The Dell, The Observatory Garden and the west side of One Tree Hill. The large pit outside the Vanbrugh gate was a substantial sand and gravel mine, largely back-filled with rubble from the Second World War. The natural pond just outside the Blackheath gate was also a gravel pit, but a lining of impervious clay has made it a pond.

Evidence of the Blackheath pebble beds is found on the high ground in places where frequent foot-fall has worn away the grass. You will see many relatively large black rounded pebbles of the Harwich Formation mixed in with the sandy soil. These pebbles, made of flint eroded from the chalk, were formed on the ancient coast line that was once here.

There is no chalk exposed in the park, but this soft white rock is found close to the surface in the south west corner of Blackheath under the small open space called The Point, which is renowned for its view. Chalk was extracted here for many years, first by stone age man to obtain flints to make tools, and later for lime to make mortar and to spread on fields to reduce the acidity of the soil. By the middle ages mines, called dene holes, were constructed widely in South East England where a vertical shaft led to a series of underground chambers where the chalk was extracted.

The remains of this mine are known as Jack Cade's Cavern and they were once accessed by stairs as a tourist attraction and club. At the bottom of Croom's Hill, lime kilns were once operated and the road now known as Greenwich South Street was originally called Limekiln Lane.

Ecosystem

The ecology of Greenwich Park is determined by both its soil and the actions of man. It has not been a natural ecosystem since it was enclosed 600 years ago, but, in its less cultivated parts, the acidic and infertile nature of the soil creates a special landscape.

The soil in the lower northern areas of the park is more fertile as it lies on clay or alluvial deposits. These areas would have been regular wet meadowland and eventually became orchards and gardens. Today they are ecologically uninteresting, being turfed and cultivated. The same applies to the flat upper southern areas, although with their pebble and sand substrate, the poor quality soil would have originally made these dry heathland, or acid grassland when it was heavily grazed.

Image 6: Acid grassland on the escarpment.

The sandy escarpment has the most acidic underlying bedrock, good drainage, the poorest soil and the least human activity. The ridge of the escarpment east of One Tree Hill escaped the changes brought about by the great landscaping and consequently still exhibits the characteristics of an acid grassland, supporting many species typical of the habitat. Larger and less compromised acid grasslands do exist in London, but this part of the park is a compact showcase for the ecosystem.

Acid Grassland

The dry and infertile soil here means that only hardy grasses and ground hugging plants can grow and survive. It also makes it difficult for one species to dominate, leading to a rich and diverse range of flora. Very occasional mowing at specific times is used to emulate the effect of animals grazing.

Image 7: Common bent. A typical acid grassland variety.

The typical grasses found here are fine-leaved varieties, often providing subtle shades of colour such as the pink notes of common bent. They are also accompanied by small plants such as the herb sheep's sorrel which can give the grass a distinct red colouration.

An obvious characteristic of acid grassland is the abundant patches of bare sandy soil creating an environment well suited to burrowing insects.

South facing slopes are

Image 8: Sheep's sorrel.

favoured as they are warmed by the sun, and if you stop and look at the ground in these places you will see lots of insect life. This particular set of fauna is unique to acid grasslands in London and has its own name, the Thames Terrace Invertebrates.

Greenwich Park supports many of these, including several species of mining bee and its predators. Information about these is provided later under Insects.

Before Enclosure
Romans

The Romans are the earliest occupants of Greenwich Park to have left any evidence of their presence. They built a temple complex [Map: G6] on the high ground in the east now known as Queen Elizabeth's Bower, and to the south, their main road from Dover to London, Watling Street, ran across the park. There are no remains visible of either today but the model below superimposed on the landscape shows that the temple was an impressive and important landmark and would have been as visible from the Thames as the Royal Observatory is now.

Image 9: The site of the temple would have made it visible for many miles.

The remains were uncovered in 1902 when an attempt was made to locate the original course of Watling Street. It initially focussed on Queen Elizabeth's Bower which is still present on the escarpment edge at the eastern boundary of the park as an unnaturally high area. The preliminary excavations unearthed some small mosaic tiles (tesserae) and lime mortar, indicating that a significant Roman building had probably existed in the area.

A dig was rapidly organised and, at a depth of just 60 centimetres, a mosaic floor was discovered along with plaster, tiles, nails and several coins. Having confirmed an important find, subsequent excavations were carried out at short notice and these produced four hundred coins with dates from AD35 to AD423 with the distribution and dates of the coins showing that the site was large and had been in use for the entire Roman occupation of Britain.

In addition to the coins, many iron and bronze items were retrieved, such as blades and a key. There was also plenty of glassware, beads, antlers, and even the teeth from a camel. Large amounts of discarded black pottery were found in rubbish pits, but many items of high quality Samian pottery[1] were also uncovered. Roof tiles, rare tiles with inscriptions and the arm of a statue gave some idea of the grand nature of the buildings, but were not enough to determine their purpose or exact locations. It was concluded that the site had been a Roman villa.

When the dig was finished, a square set of iron railings were placed on the mound within which stood a tiny fragment of the mosaics which had been found.

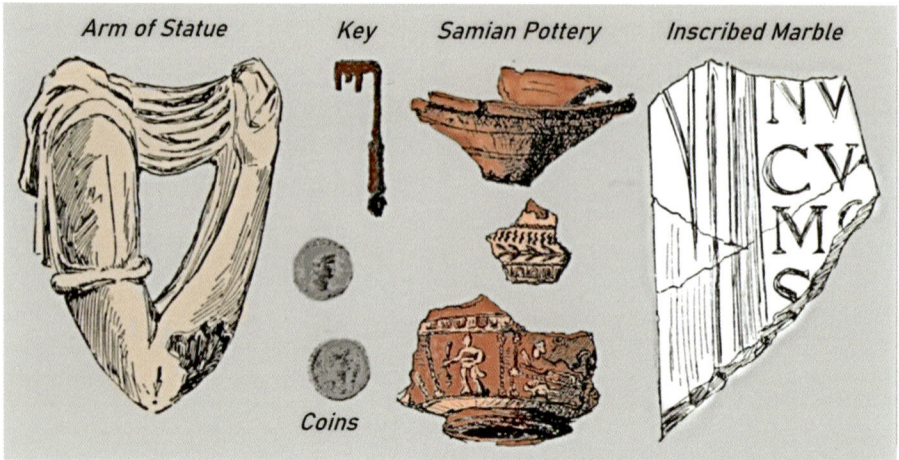

Image 10: Examples of items found in the first excavation. (PD: from A D Webster)

Image 11: The once displayed Roman remains. These are no longer present in the park.

---

1   Samian Pottery is smart red-orange decorated tableware common in Britain and used for dining. It was imported from France.

All these items are now lost or unidentifiable apart from the statue's arm and two inscribed tiles. There were no significant remains of walls found as the stone would have been taken to construct other buildings during the middle ages, but the size and weight of the roof tiles indicated that the building was substantial.

In 1999 a rapid three day excavation[2] proved to be more revealing. The foundations of walls were found and, most importantly, part of an inscribed plaque which conclusively identified that the building was a temple. The plaque was made of imported Carrara marble and had part of an inscription which could be expanded to 'IOM ET NVMINI AVG'. This showed that the temple was dedicated to Jupiter Optimus Maximus et Numini Augustus—Jupiter, the greatest of the best and the Spirit of the Emperors. It was also possible to infer that the temple had been dedicated by an individual called Lucius Caecilius Priscus.

Image 12: Fragment of the Inscription from the temple from the 1999 excavation.

Another inscription on a roof tile contained the initials PPBRL which stood for Procurator of the Province of Britannia Londinium and was evidence that at least some of the buildings had been funded by the governing military powers. Considering its position close to Watling Street and overlooking the Thames, this strengthens the likelihood that it was also linked to a fort, but no evidence of that has been uncovered.

Being a public building makes the site much more significant because it would have had many visitors. The discovery of plentiful remains of charcoal, bones and oyster shells in both digs confirms that vendors at the site were serving food to these visitors. The Romans liked shellfish and the oysters that were plentiful

---

2   Time Team UK Channel 4 Series 7 Episode 11.

along the coast of Kent were so superior to those from Italy that they were exported to Rome as a luxury delicacy despite the logistical difficulties.

Although short, this excavation was able to identify the size and location of the temple and two auxiliary buildings. Taking into account the other artefacts found, and the descriptions of contemporary buildings, it was possible to establish how the temple might have appeared.

Image 13: 3D model showing how the temple may have appeared. [created in Blender]

Watling Street

For many years it was widely accepted that the main Roman road from Dover to London, Watling Street, followed the route of the current A2 trunk road. The 1999 excavation explored other theories and confirmed that Watling Street passed through Greenwich Park providing a more direct route with a favourable gradient. The excavation showed that it was 6 metres wide and ran from a point close to Vanbrugh Park gate [Map: J7] broadly due west towards Deptford Bridge where it would have crossed the river Ravensbourne (Deptford is derived from deep ford) before heading up to London Bridge and the City of London.

Noviomagus

It is not known what name the Romans gave to the Greenwich area, but there has been some speculation that the legendary lost Roman town of Noviomagus Cantiacorum[3] (Kentish New Town) may have been in the park because of its favourable location. However, there is still no archaeological proof of this despite the uncovering of the temple. All the current evidence points to it having been on some high ground overlooking the Thames near Charlton[4]. This would have been on the minor Roman road to the north of Watling Street that ran along the Thames and which has remained a right of way continuously to this day.

There is undoubtedly far more of Britain's Roman past to be found under Greenwich Park. The temple area has not been systematically excavated and the route of Watling Street is also likely to be rich in potential finds.

---

3 A History of Greenwich, Beryl Platt. Noviomagus Cantiacorum is frequently mentioned in Roman records but its location is unknown.
4 Gilbert's Pit is a redundant gravel quarry and would have been a substantial area of high ground prior to excavation leaving nothing of archaeological value. Elliston-Erwood *Journal of the British Archaeological Association*, 1928.

Anglo-Saxons

Once the Romans had left Britain around 410 AD, the Saxons took advantage of the lack of any defence force and began to occupy the area of Kent and London. They brought with them their more primitive, rural lifestyle and had no desire to inhabit and maintain the old Roman towns or buildings. These were largely abandoned, including the temple in the park, heralding the start of the so-called dark ages.

Like previous inhabitants, the Saxons found Greenwich an ideal area to settle and called it Gronewic, or Green Bay, a name that amply reflected the safe harbour it provided set in front of the towering green woods of the escarpment on which they could safely build their homes in the dry and fertile clearings.

In the south west of the park is a feature that most visitors would hardly notice as it simply consists of a large number of low profile mounds [Map: H3]. These are between 4 and 9 metres in diameter and up to 700 centimetres high with some more pronounced than others. They would have originally stood around 2 metres high and most would have had a shallow encircling ditch, although these are barely discernible today.

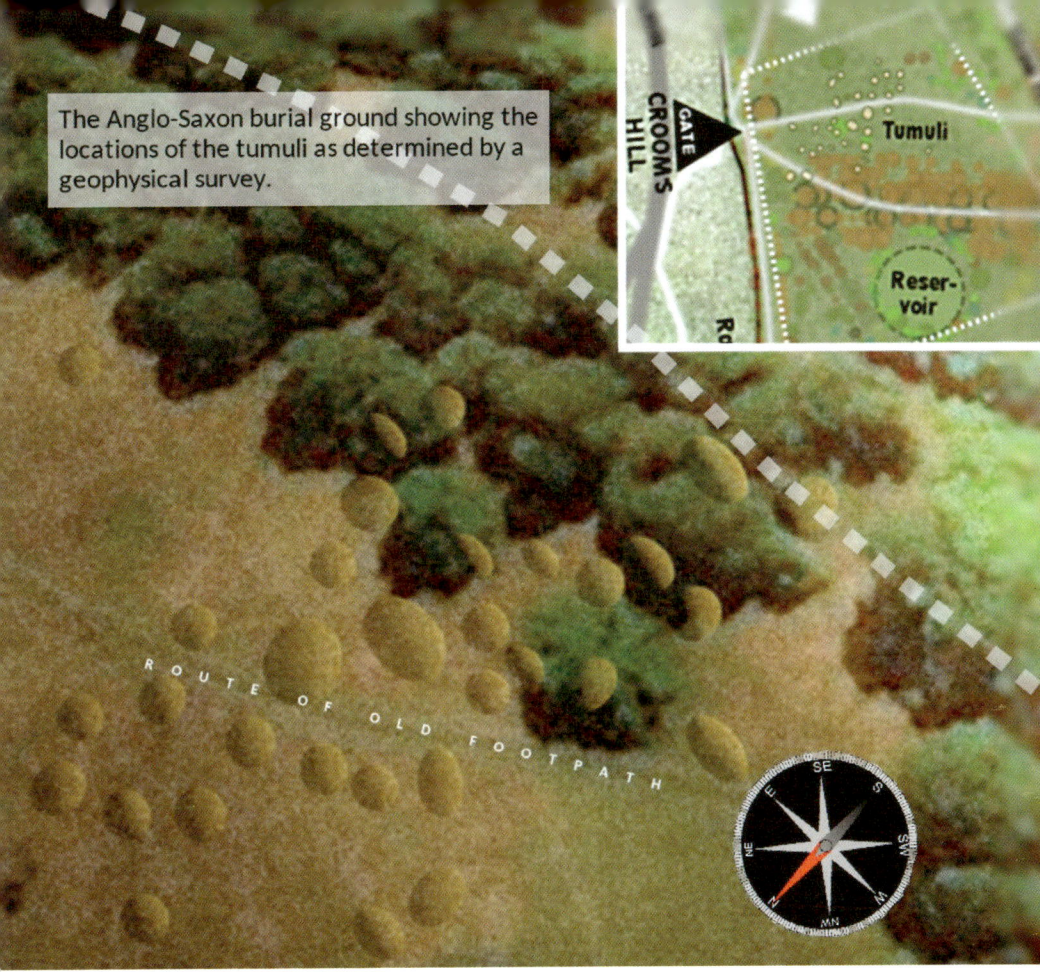

The Anglo-Saxon burial ground showing the locations of the tumuli as determined by a geophysical survey.

These mounds are Anglo-Saxon burial mounds or tumuli and, when you appreciate their age and the scale of the site, it is easy to understand why this is recognised as one of the best preserved Anglo-Saxon burial sites in the country and, as such, is legally protected.

In 1846, several tumuli were flattened during the preliminary work for the covered reservoir to the south. An enthusiastic public protest resulted in the site of the reservoir being relocated further south, saving the rest of the tumuli.

The first investigation of these tombs was at the start of the eighteenth century when a park keeper called Hearn opened several barrows and probably removed many valuable items. Unfortunately no record of what was found exists.

A more thorough excavation took place in January 1784 by the reverend James Douglas who reported that 50 barrows were opened. Like most investigations of that time, the findings were not systematically documented, however, spearheads, knives, woollen cloth, hair and fragments of human bone were uncovered along with broad headed nails still in the original wood. Most of these artefacts are now missing, but James Douglas's descriptions are still quite revealing:

The soil on which these tumuli are situated is gravel, and in some places extremely compact. The incision for the body about a foot and a half [45cm], or less, in some of them, below the surface, in the native soil; the barrow, or the conic mound of earth raised above it most probably collected from the trench, which encircles it, and from a spot of ground excavated on the east side of the range of tumuli.

Within the largest of the burrows he identified signs of a badly decomposed wooden casket that would have contained the body and from this area recovered a large iron spearhead that was almost 40cm long and 5cm wide at the socket end. This was placed where the head of the body would have laid, while at the centre was an iron dagger and parts from the central metal projection of a shield (umbo).

The barrows have been subject to several later studies and a geophysical survey in 1994[5] estimated that there were originally at least forty tumuli in the park and identified the locations of those remaining. It also concluded that the number of tombs here suggested that these were the burial locations of ordinary people and this may have been symbolic of a community that was trying to retain its old traditions during the rise of Christianity. Tumuli on Shooters Hill and in Lesnes Abbey Woods are much older than these and date back to the bronze age.

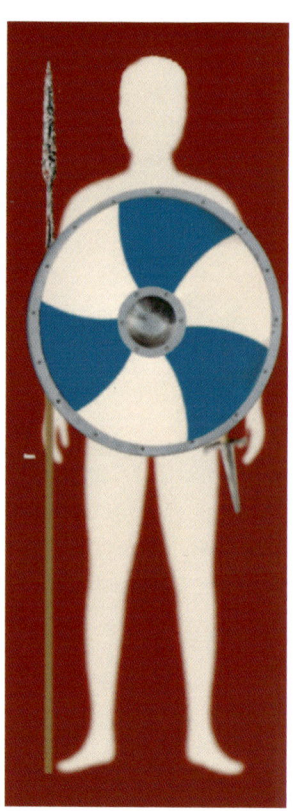

Image 14: Saxon artefacts.

---

5   Royal Commission on the Historical Monuments of England, now part of English Heritage.

Abbey of Saint Peter in Ghent

During the Anglo-Saxon era Christianity arrived in Britain, taking advantage of the reach and remains of the Roman Empire. Canterbury Cathedral was founded in 597 by Augustine close to Watling Street on the site of an old Roman church. It was overseen by an Augustine monastery and grew in stature for the next 400 years as the Roman Catholic Church came to dominate life in Britain.

The manor of Gronewic (or Greenwich), which contained the park, was listed among the possessions of King Alfred who reigned from 871 to 900. Both the manors of Lewisham and Greenwich were granted to his youngest daughter, Ælfthryth (or Elstrudis), when she married Baldwin II, the Count of Flanders. He was one of the most powerful men in Europe and a strong ally of King Alfred in his fight against the Danes.

Ælfthryth gave the rights to both manors to the Abbey of Saint Peter in Ghent on 11th September 918[6], shortly after her husband died. A satellite religious house or 'Alien House' was established and referred to as Lewisham Priory[7], but unfortunately there are no details on where this monastery would have been located.

Vikings

The Vikings, or more specifically the Danes, had been raiding the monasteries of Britain since 793 when they attacked Lindisfarne in Northumberland. Subsequently they began to settle in the north, eventually becoming so powerful that they formed a united government with the Anglo-Saxons. This restored peace, but only because the Anglo-Saxons were having to pay the Vikings annual protection money called Danegeld. By 1002 this had become such a contentious issue that King Æthelred (the unready) decided to not only stop paying the money, but to execute all the Danes living in England.

---

6   Cartularium Saxonicum, Walter de Gray Birch.
7   Monasticon Anglicanum.

In retaliation, the King of Denmark, Sweyn Forkbeard, ordered attacks against England and, in 1011, Thorkell the Tall established a base in Greenwich[8] from where he could readily pillage Kent and London. The Vikings built protective earthworks in the area that now makes up Greenwich Park and remained in control of Greenwich until 1014. Their encampment gave rise to the area being called Coombe and later Westcombe, coomb meaning camp[9].

Saint Alfege

One of Thorkell the Tall's first raids was in 1011 against the important and prestigious town of Canterbury and its cathedral. Alfege, the Archbishop of Canterbury, bravely held out against the attack for twenty days, only being captured after one of his own fearful monks let the enemy through the gates. After ransacking the cathedral, the Danes burnt it to the ground and Alfege was brought back to the Viking encampment at Greenwich in chains.

Alfege was held to ransom for six months, refusing to negotiate with the Vikings as he did not want his people to pay for his release out of their own pockets. "I am not the man to provide Christian flesh for pagan teeth by robbing my poor countrymen to enrich their enemies." The Vikings kept Alfege shackled around the ankles in a cell on the marshes leaving him in ill health and hardly able to walk. A disastrous rescue attempt failed as he simply could not keep up with his would-be liberators as they waded through the sodden ground. He was quickly recaptured and refused to name those who had sought to free him, insisting that his escape had been orchestrated solely by the devil.

This event brought things rapidly to a climax. At a feast on Easter Day, 19th April 1012, his captors became drunk and went to taunt Alfege and demand their gold. Alfege ignored their angry shouts and replied by calmly quoting passages from the bible. Legend has it that the final straw was when he calmly said: "The gold I give you is the word of God." Frustrated, drunk and incensed by his reply, his captors pelted him with bones from the feast and beat him with the handles of their axes, intending to silence him.

---

8   Old and New London: Volume VI, Edward Walford.
9   Unlike now, Westcombe was within the park and Eastcombe at Maze Hill.

Alfege was almost sixty years old and the beating was so severe and prolonged that one of the Vikings, who had converted to Christianity as a result of Alfege's evangelism, killed him outright with a blow from his axe as an act of mercy.

Image 15: The death of Saint Alfege.

News of his death spread rapidly through Christendom, together with reports of a miracle where an old rotten oar that had been driven into his body had sprouted new shoots. He was canonised in 1078 and the 19th of April declared as St Alfege's Day. A tomb to the martyr Saint Alfege was built in the new Canterbury Cathedral and in Greenwich, reputedly on the site of his cell, a church was built [Map: C1]. The current St. Alfege's is the third church of that name, but all have stood at the same location with the altar marking the place of his death.

The leader of the Vikings, Thorkell the Tall, had been coming to terms with Christianity and was outraged by the murder, fearing that he had lost control of his men. With a number of loyal followers he took 45 boats and sided with the English king, Æthelred, vowing to protect London and Kent from further attacks by the Danish. When the Danes landed in Northern England and marched on London, Thorkell helped Æthelred escape to Normandy. Sweyn became King of England in 1013, followed by his son Cnut of 'holding back the tide' fame[10].

Æthelred's seventh son, Edward, had also fled with his mother, Emma, to her homeland of Normandy. In 1016 he visited the Abbey of Saint Peter in Ghent and vowed to restore its rights to the manor of Greenwich, even though he was only twelve and had no realistic prospect of ever becoming King of England. However,

---

10 Cnut did not believe he could hold back the tide. He staged the event to demonstrate to his sycophantic followers that he was not the 'all-powerful' leader they thought he was.

in 1041, backed by the Normans, he successfully invaded and reclaimed the throne of England from the Danes, becoming Edward the Confessor. Three years later, in 1044, he authorised a charter that reaffirmed the rights to the manors of Lewisham and Greenwich to the Abbey of Saint Peter.

Saxon Hall

Image 16: Impression of Anglo Saxon manor house at sunrise.

Saxon buildings, even great halls, were usually constructed of timber with thatched roofs and so little evidence of them ever remains. This would be especially so at Greenwich where so much rebuilding has taken place. Documentation indicates that King Alfred had a manor house in Greenwich and it is likely to have been slightly east of the current Old Royal Naval College.

After the invasion of England by William the Conqueror in 1066, England was divided up and Bishop Odo became Lord of Greenwich. The Doomsday Book records that King Harold was the Earl of Greenwich prior to the conquest, confirming that he had a manor house there, likely that built by King Alfred.

The Normans

The Normans were exceptionally devout Christians, and after their successful invasion of England, they honoured the charter of Edward the Confessor and Greenwich remained an ecclesiastical outpost, or Alien House, for the Abbot of Saint Peter's Abbey who received all the taxation and tolls from the land.

In 1071, despite interventions by the Normans, Robert the Frisian seized power in Flanders and the Abbot of Ghent was forced to grant him the rights to Greenwich. It took until 1222 for the manor of Greenwich to return to the ownership of the Abbey of Saint Peter after a legal case reaffirmed their rights.

Old Court

Needing to fulfil its obligation to provide hospitality in Greenwich, the Abbey of Saint Peter built a substantial manor house by the river to replace the old Saxon building. This became known as Old Court.

Image 17: An impression of a typical monasterial lodging house from the time of Old Court.

This building is recorded in documents held in the Ghent state archives of 1286 which show that the Abbey was paying for repairs to both the building and its water supply which relied on conduits under Greenwich Park. They were also receiving payment from guests.

Old Court would have been a very important feature of Greenwich, particularly for those travelling towards London on the Thames. It served as a well-provided guest house with ten bedrooms, two kitchens and ample stabling. Guests included the abbots of other monasteries[11] and even kings. Edward I visited Greenwich and stayed here in 1300, making an offering to the holy crosses in the Chapel of the Virgin Mary.

Old Court was a substantial building and was effectively paid for by the people of Greenwich through the taxes and tolls that the Abbey collected. Resentment of this grew, and several times the king and courts were involved in disputes, particularly regarding the road tolls.

The King seizes the land

In 1337 Edward III began a war with France, later to be known as the Hundred Years' War. He was persuaded by the residents of Greenwich that because of its views over the Thames, the land of the Alien House was of such strategic significance, that it could not remain in the hands of the Flemish who were allies of the French. Edward took control of the land and appointed his own abbots to run the priory. Old Court was not well maintained and even stripped of some of its assets.

Henry IV had made Eltham palace his preferred residence, but in 1408 he was recuperating from illness and found fresh air to be helpful. He began spending more time at the recently refurbished Old Court, establishing Greenwich as a regular royal residence for the first time.

In 1414 Henry V decided to found Sheen Priory in Richmond and, to fund this, he dissolved all the Alien Houses in England, including Greenwich. He gave the manors of Greenwich and Lewisham to Sheen Priory as a source of income, but retained the manor of Old Court and granted it for life to his trusted second-in-command Thomas Beaufort, the Duke of Exeter. Beaufort died there in 1417, leaving it vacant.

---

11 St. Peter's Abbey, Ghent by Julian Watson, Greenwich Historical Society.

When Henry V died in 1422, his son, Henry VI, was just nine months old. Henry had willed his older brother, John, Duke of Bedford, to be regent and appointed his youngest brother, Humphrey, Duke of Gloucester, as Lord Protector of his son.

To be close to his ward, Humphrey took ownership of Old Court and moved in making Greenwich his home and, more importantly, went on to enclose the land that now makes up Greenwich Park. When John died unexpectedly, Humphrey assumed the role of monarch.

Image 18 Lesnes Abbey Woods. Probably similar to Greenwich Park before enclosure.

Humphrey, Duke of Gloucester

Humphrey, Duke of Gloucester, was the fourth and youngest son of King Henry IV and Mary de Bohun. This bloodline linked him to Greenwich through both the House of Flanders and the Saxon kings of England.

He was a man of books[12] and was considered to be one of the great European intellectuals by his contemporaries. His exploits in battle against the French meant he was also highly regarded by his brother, Henry V, as a soldier. He led the successful attack on the town of Harfleur, before playing a decisive role in the battle of Agincourt, gaining widespread popularity.

Image 19: Humphrey, Duke of Gloucester.

Following his acquisition of Old Court, he began drawing up plans to create a new palace. Between 1433 and 1437 he was spending as much time as he could overseeing the conversion of Old Court into a new modern palace that he named Bella Court. This included acquiring approximately 200 acres of land as a private park.

Petitions to create the park were read to Parliament on 30th January 1433 and again on 6th March 1437, when Humphrey sought to confirm his rights and allow the fortification of his houses and construction of a castle. Part of the second petition is shown below.

May it please the king our sovereign lord that from his special grace, and with the assent of his lords spiritual and temporal and of the commons assembled in this present parliament, to grant a licence to Humphrey, Duke of Gloucester, and his wife Eleanor to enclose 200 acres of their land, pasture, wood, heath, thicket and gorse, and to make a park in Greenwich thereof; and by the same authority to make towers there of stone and lime according to the form and tenor of a schedule attached to this present bill, without fee or fine to be paid to you for this[13].

---

12 His book collection formed the Bodleian Library at Oxford University.
13 Petitions in Parliament (Henry VI 1437).

Much of the land was given to him by Henry VI (who would have been just 11 years old) and had been previously bequeathed to Sheen Priory. Humphrey did not want public rights of way running through his park and so was not greedy in adopting neighbouring areas, such as West Combe, which would have required this. He duly received permission to move the paths and roads that did run through the park.

The main change would have been that Watling Street was rerouted to the southern boundary of the park from where it could then join the existing busy thoroughfare that ran down Croom's Hill on the park's western boundary. The route up the eastern side of the park that is now known as Maze Hill would have been created as a new road to replace other routes traversing the land. The local road from Deptford to Woolwich that ran along the northern boundary of the park had existed as a significant right of way since before Roman times and had to be retained as it could not easily be diverted. This road separated the park from the palace.

By the time Bella Court was finished in 1437, the new park had been enclosed with a wooden fence. The boundaries set then are broadly the same as those of Greenwich Park today. Having fenced in his land and created a beautiful, but relatively modest, red brick and white stone palace fronting the river, Humphrey also went on to build a simple crenulated tower at the highest point of the park, his castle. So it was Humphrey, Duke of Gloucester who created Greenwich Park and established the first royal palace in Greenwich.

Although he was popular with both the people of Greenwich and the country, he looked after his own interests very well and had many enemies. One was Cardinal Henry Beaufort of the long-serving Beaufort family which had previously owned Old Court. He had been chancellor during the reign of Henry V, but was forced from office by Humphrey when he became acting regent. An even greater enemy was the queen of Henry VI, Margaret of Anjou, who was very unhappy at the hold on power he retained even after Henry VI had become of age in 1437.

Image 20: Eleanor Cobham and Humphrey, Duke of Gloucester. Liber Benefactorum, from St Albans Abbey which he founded. PD

Humphrey's downfall began with his second marriage to Eleanor Cobham, who had been his mistress for many years. She shared his enthusiasm for intellectual pursuits and, as many did at the time, dabbled in alchemy, astrology and necromancy.

Humphrey's enemies used this against her in 1441 finding her guilty of treason. It was alleged that she had asked two astrologers and a witch to forecast the future health of Henry VI. Before her arrest, she fled from Greenwich and managed to gain sanctuary[14] in Westminster Abbey where the Church commuted her death sentence to penance and life imprisonment. Once she had performed a humiliating semi-naked walk through London holding a candle, she was imprisoned at Chester castle. The astrologers and witch were executed.

There was little Humphrey could do in such a situation other than accept that the balance of power had changed. The queen and Beauforts continued to conspire against him, and, after being summoned to Bury on 23rd February 1447, he was also arrested on grounds of treason. The same night he was found dead in his prison cell, almost certainly the result of being poisoned.

Margaret of Anjou hastily went to parliament, which voted to strip him and his heirs of their rights. Once done, she took ownership of Bella Court, the delightful palace in Greenwich, which she had coveted ever since spending her honeymoon there.

---

14 The law of the Catholic Church took precedence over the common law of the king and no-one could be arrested or tried in a church other than by the church authorities.

Image 21: An artistic impression of how Bella Court may have looked from the Thames based on contemporary buildings. It was not palatial and consisted of several separate parts, some of which were crenelated. The buildings facing the park were surrounded by sunny gardens that created a country ambience.

Pleasaunce

Margaret of Anjou was only seventeen when she took ownership of Bella Court and its park. She clearly thought it special as she renamed it Pleasaunce, meaning pleasant, and began to update the buildings, adding new courts and lavishly redecorating her apartments. Margaret was the first queen to take a liking to Greenwich, but certainly not the last.

Henry VI, who was very weak and mentally unstable, fell under the control of bad advisors, becoming very unpopular with the population who were being heavily taxed and driven into starvation.

The peasants revolt of 1450 saw Jack Cade march on London demanding justice for the poor. The peasants grouped on Blackheath, just beyond the park gates, before moving on to London Bridge. Unfortunately the peaceful and popular march became unruly once London was reached and many of the rebels began looting. The king's advisors sought a quick and peaceful resolution and the rebels were all promised pardons as long as they left.

However, once the rebels had left, these terms were immediately revoked by Henry VI and Jack Cade and the other leaders were hunted down, tried and executed. At the north east corner of Blackheath is a viewpoint called 'The Point' under which are chalk caverns often referred to as Jack Cade's Caverns because, legend has it, he hid there during his escape[15].

Six months after the rebellion on 23 February 1451 Henry VI made the men of Greenwich kneel before him on Blackheath to beg his pardon. This took place just beyond the park gates and, in a strange spectacle of theatre, he forced them to be naked, apart from a shift. His increasingly bizarre acts further alienated him and his unpopular queen from the people of England. He eventually withdrew from public life and Queen Margaret assumed complete power.

With popular support, Richard Plantagenet, the Duke of York, declared his own right to the throne and rose up against Henry VI, starting the War of the Roses. The Lancastrians were defeated ten years later in 1461 and Richard's son became King Edward IV. Shortly after his coronation, he came to Pleasaunce to hunt in what was now his park.

On 1st May 1464 Edward IV fell out with his closest supporters by secretly marrying the renowned beauty Elizabeth Woodville, a widow who already had two sons and twelve siblings. Edward made Pleasaunce hers for life and she made Greenwich her home, but by making the king grant favours and titles to all her family, she was also making powerful enemies.

The Earl of Warwick, known as the King Maker, had expected his family to be rewarded because of his critical support in putting Edward on the throne. Feeling betrayed, he instigated a short-lived coup in 1470 that reinstated Henry VI as king. Edward IV hastily fled abroad, leaving Elizabeth Woodville at Pleasaunce, pregnant with his fourth child. Like Eleanor Cobham, she had to flee to Westminster Abbey with her three daughters to seek sanctuary, giving birth to Edward's first male heir at the abbey while he was still in exile.

With Edward reinstated the following year, Elizabeth returned to Greenwich and Pleasaunce and bore Edward six more children. In 1481 the pope gave Edward IV

---

15   This cavern is now sealed, but for many years it was run as a tourist attraction and libertine club until closed permanently in 1854.

permission to found a house for the Observant Friars directly to the west of Pleasaunce and a year later the Bishop of Norwich laid the first stone to mark the start of construction on an old playing field.

Edward had become quite ill and died in 1483 before his new convent was complete. His young son became Edward V, but in an action made infamous by Shakespeare, his uncle, Richard III, seized the throne and locked up twelve year old Edward V and his brother Richard in the Tower of London. Elizabeth Woodville had to leave Pleasaunce again and sought sanctuary in Westminster Abbey as she had done before, leaving only when Richard III swore on oath to give her a position at court and guarantee both her safety and that of her daughters. Elizabeth returned to Greenwich, but her sons, Edward and Richard, were never seen again.

Henry VII defeated Richard III at the battle of Bosworth in 1485 and the Lancastrian Tudor's were returned to the throne on condition that he marry Elizabeth of York, Elizabeth Woodville's eldest daughter, and the legitimate heir to the throne. Henry VII took an immediate interest in the palace at Greenwich and quickly reaffirmed the charter of the Observant Friars. With the buildings now ready, he opened the convent, and continued to support it throughout his life.

In February 1487, Elizabeth Woodville left Greenwich and retired to Bermondsey Abbey, seemingly at Henry's direction. She spent the remaining five years of her life there in relative comfort. Henry VII made the palace at Greenwich his favoured residence and improved the tower that Humphrey had built on the hill in the park.

In 1499 he purchased 600,000 bricks to set about rebuilding Pleasaunce[16] completely. He renamed it the Palace of Placentia and it was finished in 1505 with most, if not all, of the original building being replaced. Fronting the river, it was similar in its appearance and scale to Hampton Court palace, construction of which was not begun until ten years later by Cardinal Wolsey, Henry VIII's chief advisor.

---

16   The demolition of Bella Court was made clear by excavations in 1970-1971.

Henry VIII

Henry VII's second son, Henry, had been born in the Palace of Placentia and baptised in St. Alfege's Church in 1491 as the new Church of the Observant Friars was still under construction. Henry VIII became king in 1509, his older brother having died seven years earlier. When the Palace of Westminster burned down in 1512, Greenwich suddenly became the absolute centre of royal life in London.

Palace of Placentia

Henry was just seventeen when he became king on 21st April 1509. Two months later, on 11th June, he married Catherine of Aragon in the Church of the Observant Friars next to the Palace of Placentia. Twelve days later she joined him at his coronation.

Henry VIII loved Greenwich even more than his father. The palace was modern and well appointed, and ideal for the fashionable feasts, balls and theatrical shows that he frequently staged. For daily exercise he could hunt in the park, and clearly did so frequently, as within just one year of becoming king he had to pay to restock it with deer.

Image 22: Henry VIII when he was 18 (Unknown Artist c.1509) PD

He was tall, handsome, athletic and loved sport. He built a tiltyard for jousting which was located to the east of the present day Queen's House and was around 200 metres long and 70 metres wide. He also had a real tennis court[17] built in the palace, another sport at which he excelled.

---

17   Real Tennis is played in a closed court yard and the ball can be hit against the walls.

Image 23: Henry VIII tilting in front of Katherine of Aragon, his first ex-wife.
THOMAS WRIOTHESLEY, COLLEGE OF ARMS / CC BY-SA 4.0

The various foreign ambassadors that visited the Palace of Placentia carried reports around Europe of its beauty and the extravagant events staged by the king. The contemporary poet John Leyland wrote:

Lo! with what lustre shines this wish'd-for place!
Which star-like might the heavenly mansion's grace.
What painted roofs! What windows charm the eye!
What turrets, rivals of the starry sky!
What constant springs! what verdant meads besides!
Where Flora's self in majesty resides.
And beauteous all around her, does dispense,
With bounteous hand, her flow'ry influence.
Happy the man whose lucky wit could frame,
To suit this place, so elegant a name,
Expressing all its beauties in the same.

On the 12th June, 1510 the palace at Greenwich was the location for an all-comers event where Henry could show off his prowess:

Henry VIII with two others challenged all comers to fight at the barriers with targates and casting the eight feet spear, then to fight twelve strokes with two-handed swords. In October of the same year the king prepared a stand within the park for the queen and ladies to witness a fight with battle-axes, where the king fought with Guyot, a Fleming[18].

---

18 Hall's Chronicles

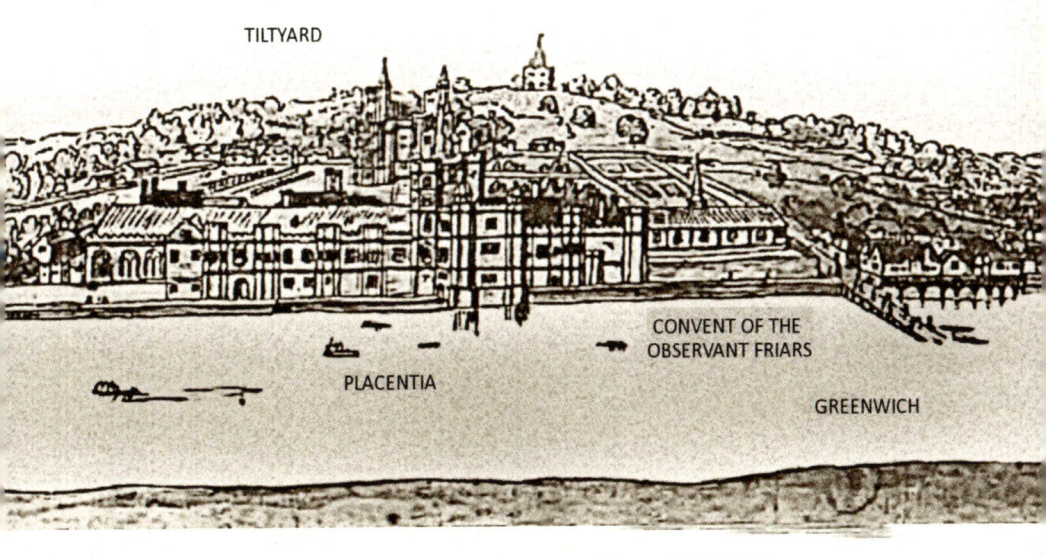

Wyngarde's panorama of Greenwich c. 1543 [PD]

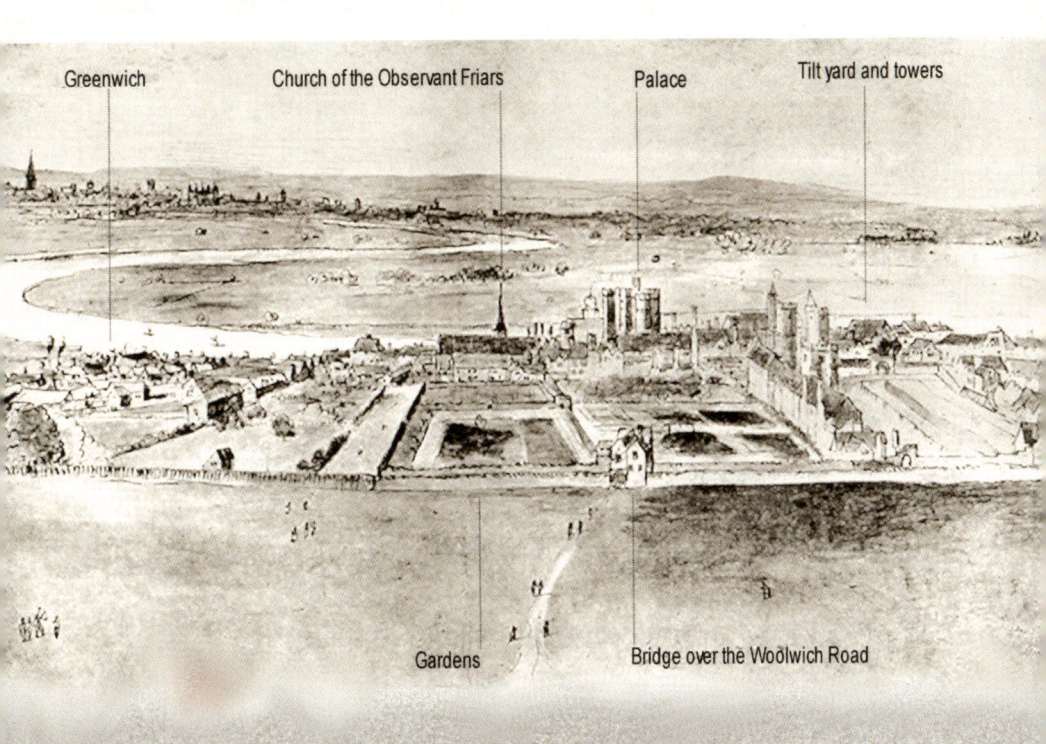

Queen Catherine fell pregnant six times, but only Mary, who was the fifth child, survived. She was born in the Palace of Placentia in 1516. After Catherine's last pregnancy of 1518 ended without producing a male heir, Henry began to seek approval for divorce. He received no support from the Catholic Church, and, more disappointingly, none from his priests, the Observant Friars, who remained loyal to the pope and to Catherine despite Henry's generous support to them over the years.

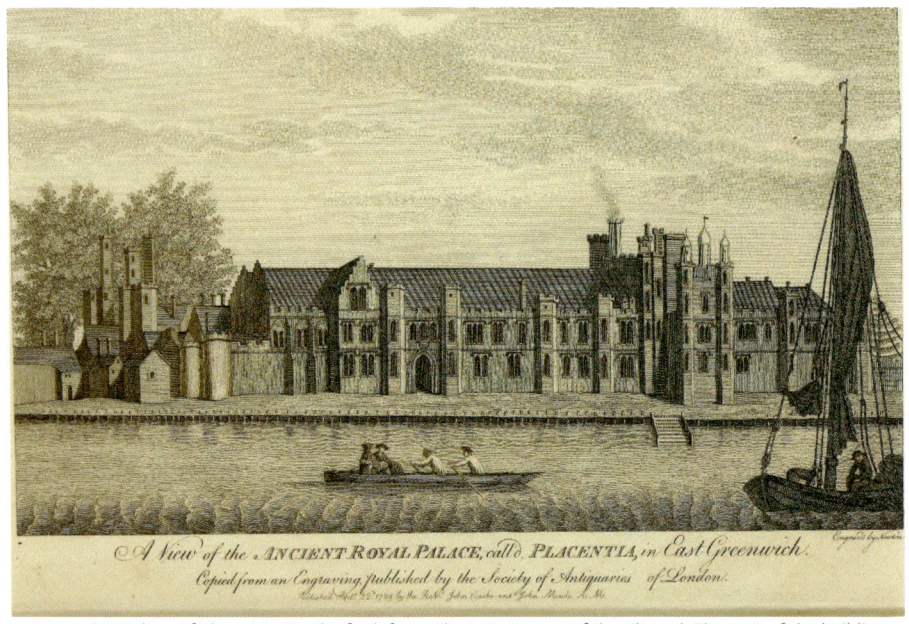

Image 24: Palace of Placentia. On the far left are the twin towers of the tiltyard. The east of the building contains the chapel and the bed chambers are on the far right. Adjacent to the steps, the privvy has a passage under it to allow the public to use the right of way along the river bank. PD

Henry VIII continued to enhance the Palace of Placentia and by 1520 the area that is now the grounds of the National Maritime Museum and the Queen's House had been laid out with formal gardens. The tiltyard had been improved with two large towers that provided seating for those watching and could even be stormed in mock battles. There were butts for archery and new buildings were constructed to support the palace including an armoury and stables. A bridge was built over the Woolwich Road[19] to allow access from the palace and

---

19   Which at that time ran where Park Vista is today, not its current route.

sports ground to the park, and this was regularly used by Henry, his family, the palace courtiers and their many guests.

In 1533, when Henry was 42 and had been married to Catherine for 24 years, he finally despaired of getting papal approval for his divorce and broke with the Catholic Church. He married Anne Boleyn whom he had courted at Greenwich, both in the palace and the park. Anne bore him a daughter, Elizabeth, on 7th September 1533 in Greenwich.

It was also in 1533 that Thomas Cromwell began gathering evidence against the Observant Friars. Henry had continued to support them, and had even had Elizabeth baptised in their church, but they refused to acknowledge him as the Supreme head of the Church in England. With Cromwell's evidence he expelled them from the Convent. They continued to oppose him while in-hiding around the country, but Henry pursued them remorselessly, tracking many of them down and having them executed as heretics.

Despite getting older and having a number of hunting accidents, Henry remained fearless and competitive in sport. However, his second jousting accident in January 1536 at the tiltyard in Greenwich, was so serious that it proved to be life changing. He was thrown from his horse in full armour and his horse, itself in armour, fell on top of him. At first it was thought he must be dead, but after remaining unconscious for two hours he eventually came round. His legs never properly recovered and he became more sedentary, piling on weight and suffering further ill health as a consequence.

Four months later, the tiltyard at Greenwich was the scene of Anne Boleyn's downfall. Unbeknown to her, Henry had asked Thomas Cromwell to investigate her conduct, and this had resulted in the arrest of three men accused of sleeping with her, one being her brother. During a joust on May Day that she was watching with Henry, he angrily stormed out of the event having received a message that one of those arrested had confessed to the charges. Stories about her being caught dropping a handkerchief at the joust for one of her lovers to pick up were invented later to damage her reputation[20].

---

20 The handkerchief had become popular around this time and the dropping and giving of a handkerchief to a man was deemed to be highly flirtatious.

The next day Anne was taken by barge from Greenwich to the Tower of London and she was executed seventeen days later. Henry married his third wife, Jane Seymour, the day after Anne's execution, but she herself died a year later after giving birth to his only son.

In 1540, his latest bride, Anne of Cleves, was met by Henry VIII on Blackheath at a lavish re-enactment of the 'Field of the Cloth of Gold'[21], and conveyed through the park to the palace, preceded by trumpets and kettle-drums, and followed by all the nobles. They entered by the Blackheath gate, passed through the park to the north west gate and through the town, by way of Friar's Road, to the Palace. Even Greenwich Castle played a part with 'a peal of guns being shot out from the tower in the park.'

Image 25: Henry VIII around 1540. PD

To set up his son, Edward, for succession, he signed the Treaty of Greenwich with the Scots at the Palace of Placentia in 1543. Within this treaty Edward was formally betrothed to Mary Queen of Scots to unite the two kingdoms. However, the Scots reneged on the conditions of the treaty the same year and a bloody war ensued led by Jane Seymour's brother, Edward Seymour. Henry continued to live at Greenwich, although he had begun spending much more time at the new Hampton Court Palace that he had seized from Cardinal Wolsey following his execution.

Henry died in 1547 at Whitehall and Edward VI, who was only nine, was crowned king with Edward Seymour, now Duke of Somerset, as Lord Protector. In 1553 Edward became seriously ill and took permanent residence in Greenwich to benefit from the air. His closest advisors feared a radical return to Catholicism if

---

21 Henry VIII's famous meeting with Francis I at Calais in a field where he demonstrated his wealth and power by the use of many gilded tents.

he should die and Mary become queen, and began plotting immediately to prevent this. Edward VI was only fifteen, terminally ill and in pain, but he was kept alive by the palace physicians with arsenic. So that the people of Greenwich could see him, and report that he was still living, he was made to stand in a window that overlooked the path in front of the palace.

Looking weaker and more gaunt every day, Edward VI died before the plans for the alternative succession were complete and, after delaying the announcement of his death for four days, Lady Jane Grey[22] was hastily proclaimed queen. The conspirators had unfortunately misjudged the mood of the country, and this coup proved to be even more unpopular than the prospect of being ruled by Mary. Just nine days later Mary was made queen and those who had sought to deny her the throne, including Lady Jane Grey, were executed.

Mary I

For five years the Palace of Placentia remained largely unoccupied as Queen Mary had no great love for it, but her religious fervour meant that one of her first acts as queen was to undo one of her father's wrongs and reinstate the Convent of the Observant Friars.

Mary I undertook a vicious and retaliatory persecution of protestants after the passing of the Heresy Act in 1555. The Gloucester Arms public house which is situated opposite Saint Mary's gate once contained Greenwich prison and during Mary's reign wealthy protestants who refused to renounce protestantism were incarcerated there in chains, along with common criminals.

As hatred of her increased, the Observant Friars even wrote to her complaining that they had been pelted with stones by the town's folk while they were walking in the streets of Greenwich.

On her death on the 17th November 1558, a bonfire was lit in the park and there was great rejoicing across the country.

---

22 A granddaughter of Henry VII.

Elizabeth I

With Elizabeth I as queen, Greenwich was once again the favourite Royal palace, alive with music, dances, lavish entertainment and international ceremonies. She made full use of the park and some events of 1559 were recorded contemporaneously by Henry Machyn, the diarist, in A London Provisioner's Chronicle:

[On the morning of the second of July an army, formed of members of the guilds of London,] removed toward Greenwich to the court there and thence into Greenwich Park. Here they tarried till eight o'clock. And then they marched down into the lawn. And there they mustered in harness, all the gunners in shirts of mail. And at five o'clock at night the Queen came into the gallery of the park gate, and the ambassadors and lords and ladies, to a great number, and my lord marquis and my lord admiral, and my Lord Dudley and divers more lords and knights. And they rode to and fro to view them and to set the two battles in array. And after came trumpeters blowing on both parts and the drums and flutes. And three onsets in every battle. They marched forward and so the guns shot and the morris pikes encountered together with great alarm and after recoiled back again. And there the Queen's Grace thanked them heartily, and all the City. And immediately there was the greatest shout that ever was heard and hurling up of caps that Her Grace was so merry. For there was above a thousand people beside the men that mustered. And after, there was running at the tilt. And after, everyone home to London and other places.

The tenth day of July was set up in Greenwich Park a goodly banqueting house made with fir poles and decked with birch and all manner of flowers, both of the field and gardens, as roses, gillyflowers, lavender, marigolds, and all manner of strewing herbs and flowers. There were also tents for kitchens and for all officers against the morrow, with wine, ale, and beer.

The eleventh day of July there was made a place for the Queen's pensioners to run without a tilt with spears. Challengers: my Lord of Ormond, Sir John Perrot, and Mr. North. And there were ... defenders, both with spears and swords. About five o'clock at afternoon the Queen's Grace came and the ambassadors and divers lords and ladies stood over the park gate for to see. And after, they ran, one chasing the other. And after, the Queen's Grace came down into the park and took her horse and rode up to the banquet house, and the ambassadors and the lords and ladies. And so to supper. After was a masque, and after, a great banquet. And after, great casting of fire and shooting of guns till twelve at night.

Elizabeth loved riding her horse in the park and was a keen hunter. A report by the French ambassador in 1575 revealed that she had killed six does with her crossbow in just one outing.

She had one other love at Greenwich, Robert Dudley, Earl of Leicester who was her beau from her very first days as queen until he secretly married Lettice Knollys in 1576 and incurred her wrath, lucky to escape with his life.

Elizabeth's finest hour came in 1588 with her victory over the Spanish Armada. The Spanish aimed to convey a huge army of invasion up the Thames to take London and then England, restoring the country to Catholicism.

Image 26: Queen Elizabeth I, c. 1550. PD

Although good fortune played a large part in the routing of the Spanish fleet, it was the daring and novel tactics of the English navy that ultimately sealed their fate. Plymouth is most often associated with the victory, but the English navy had been created in the Greenwich area by Henry VII and then Henry VIII. Elizabeth's Navy Board was responsible for the fleet and was located just west of the Palace of Placentia in Deptford with Sir John Hawkins as treasurer. It was here where the strategy and tactics were developed that let the English fleet outpace and outmanoeuvre their opponents so successfully.

Greenwich was the perfect home for a queen whose country now controlled the seas. Just two months after defeating the Spanish she was able to step aboard Thomas Cavendish's ship Desire from the gates of her palace for a sumptuous dinner. The ship had been equipped with sails of blue damask and was full of Spanish treasure, looted during his circumnavigation of the world[23].

---

23 He was not first, but was the fastest. Sir Francis Drake had already circumnavigated the world eight years before.

Image 27: Thomas Cavendish's ship Desire approaches the palace.

In her last years, she would have watched an ever increasing number of merchant ships plying the Thames from the windows of her palace. Each vessel brought with it goods from around the world to the rapidly expanding docks and flourishing markets in the city of London.

On 31st December 1601 she granted a Royal Charter to the East India Company, giving it exclusive rights to trade with Asia. This organisation existed for 250 years and became so powerful that its needs largely determined English foreign policy during that time.

Elizabeth had set England on its way to building the largest empire the world has ever known.

Image 28: East India Co. Coat of Arms. PD

James I and Queen Anne

The palace and the park were given to Queen Anne (Anne of Denmark) by King James I, most likely on his coronation as King of England in 1603[24] although more romantic reasons have been suggested.

Anne was a great patron of the arts and exceedingly extravagant. She had palaces at Richmond and Somerset House where she organised many social events. It seems that she took little interest In Greenwich until 1612 when she engaged her son's tutor, Salomon de Caus, and the renowned gardener John Tradescant, to improve the gardens at her palaces, including Greenwich.

All de Caus' garden designs feature sculptures and fountains that were considered spectacular in their day. His

Image 29 Queen Anne by Marcus Gheeraerts. PD

Image 31: Salomon de Cause. PD

Image 32: John Tradescant the Elder by Cornelis de Neve. PD

Image 30: Inigo Jones by William Hogarth PD

---

24 He was James VI of Scotland from 1567 and heir to the English throne.

garden at Greenwich was no exception, with visitors commenting specifically on a large and elaborate fountain as well as a grotto and an exotic bird house.[25]

Image 33: A drawing of a typical Salomon de Caus fountain very similar to one described as being in Greenwich. PD

In 1615 Queen Anne commissioned the building of the Queen's House, employing the services of Inigo Jones, whose revolutionary design resulted in the first classical Palladian building in the country. Sadly she died before it was completed.

Image 34: The Queen's House. PD

---

25 The Gardens Trust

The Naval College, Queen's House and park in the summer of 2018 during a drought.

Charles I and Henrietta Maria

In 1635, Charles I finally completed the Queen's House for his French queen Henrietta Maria. She spent extra-ordinarily sums of money on its lavish interiors rivalling those of Versailles. She even brought Orazio Gentileschi and his daughter Artemesia from Italy to paint the ceilings[26].

The Queen's House [Map: D4] was built because of the park. Half in it, and half outside, it straddled the original Woolwich Road, allowing direct access to both the park and the Palace of Placentia and its gardens. The loggia overlooked the parkland, and in a few years time the park would begin to be reshaped with the Queen's House as its focal point.

Even today the Queen's House remains imposing as the centrepiece of the view from the observatory, although when built it would have been more so, standing on its own, without the colonnades and surrounding buildings.

Image 35: Henrietta Maria,c.1630. PD

Henrietta loved Greenwich and continued to develop the gardens using the services of her head gardener John Tradescant the younger, but while journeying there in 1629, when six months pregnant, she had a fall. The local midwife was called, but fainted on discovering who it was she was treating. Charles I pleaded with his staff to save his wife which they did, but his first son died shortly after being born. Charles II was born a year later at Hampton Court, leaving Elizabeth I as the last English monarch to have been born in Greenwich.

---

26 These paintings were given to Sarah Churchill in 1708 as a present. They are now on the ceiling in Marlborough House in London.

The Commonwealth

Charles I and his wife were such prolific spenders of the county's money, and so contemptuous of parliament, that it resulted in a revolution and civil war. Having been defeated and captured, the king was tried, found guilty of treason, and executed. So in 1649 England became a republic, or commonwealth, under the leadership of Oliver Cromwell.

In 1653 Oliver Cromwell attempted to sell Placentia, the Queen's House and the park. Such luxury, built using the taxes of the poor, was an anathema to the austere puritans and against the principles of the commonwealth of the new republic of England.

A small part of it was bought by the Keeper of the house and park, Uriah Babington[27], but the rest was sold to a John Parker who then tried to sell off the land and buildings separately for a profit, an early example of property development. However, when he failed to come up with the £5,778 asking price, the Queen's House and park reverted to the Commonwealth and Babington resumed management of them. Placentia was turned into a factory for making ship's biscuits.

Image 36: Oliver Cromwell, 1653. Sir Peter Lely PD

No further efforts were made to sell the property and Parliament eventually ordered that the Queen's House must be guarded to prevent defacement and pilfering. It seems that Cromwell was won over by the beauty of the location as in 1654 he moved into the Queen's House, it having been repaired and declared fit for the Lord Protector.

---

27   Uriah Babington was Charles I's hair dresser and appointed Keeper of Greenwich house and park for life in 1634 and bought his accommodation and associated land, National Archives.

Queen's House and Greenwich Palace from One Tree Hill. Hendrick Danckerts (1625–1680).
The park is seen here after Boreman's planting with the two avenues either side of the unfinished parterre on which some deer are grazing. The single wing of Charles II's new palace by the Thames prior to its conversion into the Naval Hospital can be seen by the Thames. The high park wall running through the Queen's House is clearly visible as is the old conduit house that is integrated into the wall on the right and behind it some parts of Placentia and its gardens remain.
On the left is the village of Greenwich and the spire of the earlier St. Alfege's Church. PD

Charles II

The reinstatement of the Crown in 1660 with the ascension of Charles II resulted in a new spell of radical change for the palace and park at Greenwich.

Charles II decided to build a new palace to replace the Palace of Placentia which was in poor condition. Plans were drawn up in 1661 by John Webb for a substantial building which was to consist of two wings perpendicular to the Thames and a third building behind those creating a large courtyard facing the river [Map: B4].

Work began on construction in 1664, but was abandoned in 1669 with just the west wing built. This new palace was never occupied and was later incorporated, without change, into the Naval Hospital which largely completed the original vision[28].

While all this was in progress, the remains of Greenwich Castle were demolished and replaced by the Royal Observatory, this work being completed rapidly between 1675 and 1676.

For five years from the start of Charles II's reign in 1660, Greenwich Park was extensively relandscaped and we will look at that in detail shortly.

Image 37: Charles II. PD

---

28 Although the two wings look identical you will find decorative inscriptions to Charles II the west building above the river fronting portico: Carolus Rex II.

William and Mary

The Naval Hospital

In 1669, Mary, queen to William III (William of Orange), commissioned the building of a retirement home for infirm sailors on the site of the old Palace of Placentia. This was based on the incomplete palace constructed by Charles II which was empty. Sir Christopher Wren was the architect and oversaw construction, following the original John Webb design [Map: B4].

Image 38: Mary II, Queen of England. PD

He built an exact copy of the existing palace to the east, but Queen Mary wanted to be able to see the river from the Queen's House, and objected to the central building which would have obscured the view. Wren redesigned it to be two symmetrical halves, each with its own dome. In so doing, one of the greatest panoramas in London was created.

Image 39 Leonard Knyff, 1695. How the Naval Hospital would have looked based on Christopher Wren's original plans. PD

The Queen's House became part of the hospital in 1807 and was used to extend the existing school for the children of those in the hospital or who had died in service in the navy. The distinctive covered colonnades were added in 1809 after the park wall had been moved south to its current position to provide larger grounds for the school.

By 1821, it was educating 900 children, a third of whom were girls. In 1841 it was decided that the school would focus on naval training, including the dangerous task of rigging a tall ship. That year the girl's school was closed and a full size model of a corvette with tall masts called 'Fame' was constructed directly in front of the Queen's House providing quite a landmark for Greenwich [Map: C4].

Image 40: The training ship 'Fame' outside the Queen's House when it was a naval school. PD

When the doors of the hospital had opened in 1705 there were just 42 inmates, but by 1738 this had reached 1,000, and by 1770 over 2,000. After the Battle of Trafalgar in 1805 there was a particularly large intake of wounded and crippled sailors and by 1814 the hospital reached its full capacity of 2710 seamen. The decline in naval activity after the decisive victory of Trafalgar meant that the hospital gradually emptied and it was closed in 1869 as the Royal Navy had found a new use for it.

The Royal Naval College

The hospital was converted into a Naval College using the existing buildings with little modification being necessary. Evidence of its time as the Naval Hospital can still be found in many places in the form of its distinctive coat of arms with four anchors surrounded by a rope.

The dining room, now known as the Painted Hall because of its remarkable painted ceilings by Sir James Thornhill, had been converted into a gallery for the hospital's extensive art collection. The hospital residents were moved downstairs to eat in the undercroft, where you can also find their bowling alley, still in working order.

Image 41: The arms of the Naval Hospital still adorn the Old Royal Naval College. These being on the water gate facing the Thames.

With the arrival of the Naval College, dining returned to the Painted Hall, the paintings still decorating the walls. The complete art collection was eventually handed over to the National Maritime Museum on its foundation in 1939 so they could be put on public display. The Naval College was in use until 1998 when it was given to a newly formed charity to look after and maintain the buildings.

These days it houses Greenwich University and the renowned Trinity Laban Conservatoire of Music and Dance. It also allows visitors into the quite remarkable painted hall and chapel. The old engineering workshop contains a tourist office and small museum about the history of Greenwich and its palaces [Map: B3].

Some remains of the old Tudor palace exist under the painted hall where they can be seen, and also under the Queen Anne building where the public are not generally allowed.

Today the old buildings and observatory are museums and a university. The park is owned and managed by a charity, The Royal Parks. The view towards the park from the other side of the Thames has scarcely changed since it was captured by Canaletto in 1750. PD

The Great Landscaping

Greenwich Park was originally a game park and primarily used for hunting, whilst also providing firewood and other natural resources to the palace. The park you see today was reshaped by extensive landscaping and replanting in the seventeenth century.

Hunting

In the Tudor era hunting was not just the sport of kings, it was also the favoured form of exercise for the aristocracy, and a deer park was the ultimate status symbol of the time.

It is worth noting that apart from the blowing of horns and barking of dogs, hunting would have been a lot quieter than today as the preferred weapon was the crossbow. Although guns were available, and were used in battle, they were not accurate enough or light enough for hunting and could certainly not be fired while mounted on a horse.

Image 42: Hunting Deer from 'The Master of Game' .PD

Good hunting meant that a kill was neither too difficult, nor too easy, as this made it challenging and enjoyable. There needed to be the right amount of cover and open space, and, since it was often an all day event there was also a need for pleasant locations where the participants could rest and enjoy an alfresco lunch. Greenwich Park with its gulleys, hills and views was almost perfect, explaining its popularity.

The park would have looked very different to how it does now and the description of the land enclosed by Humphrey, Duke of Gloucester, confirms that it was similar to modern southern heathland areas that have escaped urbanisation. There would have been plenty of wild deer that would have kept the tree growth in check as they grazed, making it fairly easy to maintain. A clearing at the top of the escarpment in Lesnes Abbey Woods a few miles to the east of Greenwich Park, and previously illustrated, is probably a very close approximation to how the park would have looked with bushes, gauze, heather and few young trees.

By the start of the seventeenth century the old style of hunting park was no longer considered fashionable and James I decided to replant the park with new trees and shrubs. His queen, Anne of Denmark, engaged Salomon de Caus for a year in 1612 to design the garden at Greenwich and, being strongly influenced by the current trends in gardening, he would have followed the work of Claude Mollet who had made Italian garden design fashionable with the French kings.

By as early as 1614 the park was described as looking like a garden when viewed from the high ground, with tall poplar trees lining the various avenues. Work on the Queen's House for Anne of Denmark had begun in 1616 and in 1619 James I began replacing the wooden fence around the park with a much more substantial brick wall. There are several references to Claude Mollet's son, André, being in England the following year and working for James I[29]. Although he would have been only twenty, he and his brother were becoming recognised leaders in landscape gardening throughout Europe.

André Mollet went on to make a name for himself as the designer of the Tuileries gardens in Paris and those at the Chateau of Fontainebleau. He had already produced several drawings of garden designs when he was younger and some of these were included in a book produced by his father. However, he was most notable for being the first person to advocate that avenues should be the primary feature of a garden.

---

29   André knew Salomon de Caus's son, Isaac, who was working at Wilton House and seems to also be acquainted with Inigo Jones. Some texts suggest he was in London between 1620 and 1625.

The first adornment of a royal palace should be a grand double avenue or triple row of elms or limes which ought to be laid out at right angles with the front of the house. At the beginning of the avenue there should be a large semicircle or square so that the general design can be better observed. Then at the back of the house there should be constructed parterres en broderie near it so that they can easily be enjoyed from the windows without any obstacles of trees, palisades or any other high objects that might impede the eye from seeing their full extent.

After the death of James I, Charles I and his queen, Henrietta Maria, employed André Mollet on and off from 1629 to design royal gardens, laying out those at Wimbledon Manor during 1641. His skills were much in demand, and by 1646 he had moved permanently to Stockholm to become head gardener for the King of Sweden. He eventually returned to England to become the royal gardener to Charles II, but not until 1661 when he was in his sixties. During this time he developed St. James park with canals, tree lined avenues and the circular junctions called patte d'oie, but it was also at this time that Greenwich Park was being dramatically reshaped.

Image 43: The edge of Great Cross Avenue . Chestnut trees line the outside and limes the inside. The lime trees would have originally been elms but the layout is the same as the original planting.

Seventeenth Century Replanting

It is Charles II who is primarily responsible for the layout of the park today. He was heavily influenced by his mother, Henrietta Maria, and his sister, Henrietta Anne, who had both lived in the Queen's House and then looked after him at various French palaces while they were exiled in France during the commonwealth. When he became king in 1660 he took a great interest in the palace at Greenwich and in August 1661 he agreed to a request by William Boreman, the manager of the palace and park, to begin replanting trees to meet the everyday needs of the palace. Not only had many been chopped down, but the deer, which were no longer being hunted for sport, were eating all the new saplings.

Boreman, who was not a gardener, firstly concentrated the planting in fourteen large coppices located in the south of the park in the area now known as The Wilderness [Map: K6]. Orchards were also added nearer to the palace, and a revived example of one of these can be seen in the recently renovated Queen's Orchard in the north east corner of the park. With encouragement from his mother and sister, Charles II requested Boreman oversee a major replanting and landscaping of the park along the lines of the French gardens he had seen.

It is unlikely that the routes of the seven main avenues changed significantly from those created for James I by Claude Mollet since they were constrained by the contours and boundaries of the park and the position of the Queen's House. The Keeper's Cottage, located on the escarpment next to Queen Elizabeth's Oak [Map: G5], was also retained, further restricting the opportunity to relocate the avenues.

As previously mentioned, André Mollet was back in England in 1661 working for Charles II landscaping St. James Park, and would have no doubt had some influence on this work. Three of the avenues, including the main Eltham Avenue, converged at the Blackheath gate in a large semicircular patte d'oie [Map: L4]. This is very characteristic of Mollet's designs, but it has largely been lost with the various changes around the gate to accommodate the lodge and other buildings. Even the avenue that ran to the north west is no more.

Boreman began replanting the avenues, firstly using hundreds of Spanish chestnuts sourced from nearby Lesnes Abbey, and then hundreds of elms. Elms or limes were the favoured innermost trees for avenues at that time. Boreman had also levelled the land at the end of Eltham Avenue next to the ruins of the castle to create a large terrace [Map: F4]. At the same time he carved out smaller terraces into the escarpment beneath it. Each was 40 metres long and from a distance they looked like giant steps. Scots pine trees were brought from Scotland and planted at the ends of each terrace to enhance them. The diarist, Samuel Pepys, visited the park on the 11th April 1662 and wrote:

Sir William [Penn] and I walked into the parke, where the king hath planted trees and made steps in the hill up to the Castle, which is very magnificent.

While Boreman was busy planting, Charles II was looking for someone to help complete his vision for the palace gardens in a spectacular style and his sister, Henrietta Anne, recommended that her brother engage the services of André Le Nôtre. He had become head gardener of the Claude Mollet designed Tuileries' gardens in Paris in 1637 and redesigned them. By 1655 his style had proved so desirable that he was elevated to the status of head gardener by Louise XIV, taking over the role from Claude Mollet. He was tasked with creating the gardens for the palace of Versailles in 1662, but was also asked to work on many other gardens for the French king at the same time.

Charles II invited André Le Nôtre to Greenwich in May 1662 to draw up designs for Greenwich Park, but it is not believed that he actually ever visited England as Louis XIV was keeping him extremely busy. He was, however, provided with maps and drawings of Greenwich Park and a briefing document, and from these drew up some plans which focussed on the creation of a formal garden, or parterre, on the low ground in front of the Queen's House. Since we know that Boreman had completed the landscaping of the rest of the park at this time, the parterre was the only area that needed completion.

Since the fashion at the time was that the garden should be thought of as an extension of its house, the Queen's House was to be the greatest influence on the design and the symmetry of the park, and was already located on the centre line of Eltham Avenue.

The parterre was to contain sunken gardens, fountains and, at the back, a grotto made up of seven arches. The giant steps were to form a central feature with the grotto incorporated in the step at the bottom.

The avenues would radiate from the parterre to the four walls of the park [Map: E4].

During 1663, Charles II seconded gardeners from Hampton Court to work at Greenwich on the new parterre. It was painstakingly levelled by manually moving almost 150,000 tonnes of soil[30] and the extent of this can still be seen clearly today. The following year thousands of new trees were planted along the new and existing avenues, their care continuing into the summer of 1665, at which point the development of the gardens was abruptly halted.

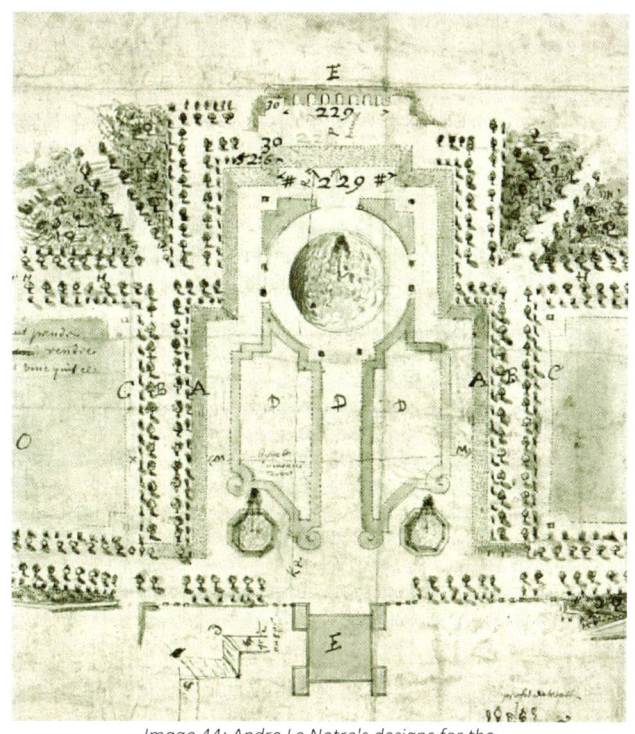

Image 44: Andre Le Notre's designs for the parterre in Greenwich Park. At the bottom is the Queen's House and a grotto is sited at the top opposite it, which is 229 feet long (70m). PD

Although not part of Le Nôtre's drawings, Charles II had decided that there was to be a grand cascade flowing down the great steps as the focal point of the design. Correspondence between Charles II and his sister in Paris show that he wanted Le Nôtre to include this cascade in some new plans, assuring his sister, as intermediary, that there would be an adequate water supply to support it.

Blackheath did not capture anywhere near enough water for a cascade and, although water could have been brought to Blackheath from Shooters Hill, the construction of a conduit four kilometres long would have been extremely costly.

---

30 Estimated from the records of Edward Maybancke, the contractor for this work.

Image 45: The cascade at the Villa Aldobrandini. Close to Rome it was a papal garden built around 1600. The water features were fed by an 8km long aqueduct. PD

Not only that, but the water from the springs of Shooters Hill was very rich in minerals making it unsuitable for a cascade and fountains. The lack of this feature was clearly a deal breaker for Charles II and he could see no point in continuing[31]. Thwarted in his attempts to create his own Versailles, Charles II abandoned the plan for the parterre leaving just the shaped and levelled area of parkland in front of the Queen's House. Hampton Court became his preferred palace and he left Sir William Boreman to oversee the management of the park at Greenwich where, in 1671, he was appointed underkeeper of both the Queen's House and the park.

For Greenwich Park and for Greenwich itself, this abandonment of the gardens turned out to be extremely fortuitous, for instead of building fountains, cascades and a copy of Versailles, Charles II found himself interested in the challenges of navigation and needed somewhere to build a new observatory to measure the stars. He ordered the replacement of the crumbling Greenwich Castle with Sir Christopher Wren's iconic Royal Observatory, an act that eventually placed Greenwich at the centre of the world [Map: E4].

---

31   Garden Works In Greenwich Park: 1662-1728 by David Jacques

The most obvious remnants of the great landscaping are the many straight, tree lined avenues, the most impressive of which is the one that runs from Blackheath to the observatory and was originally called Eltham Avenue because it led towards the palace at Eltham. The parterre planned by Le Nôtre in front of the Queen's House is a large flat area criss-crossed by paths and popular for ball games. Its flattened shape is still visible on careful inspection, with the two parallel avenues either side being slightly elevated, especially at the back.

Although the design of Greenwich Park is usually attributed to the more famous André Le Nôtre, the only link to his involvement are the plans for the unfinished parterre. Sir William Boreman created the avenues, and limitations imposed by the escarpment and existing features meant that these almost certainly followed the designs of Claude Mollet that were implemented under James I. André Mollet, who was employed by Charles II at the same time as Boreman was landscaping, would have also indirectly had some influence over this work.

Greenwich Park c.1665

A Boreman's Wilderness

B Mollet's patte d'oie

C Boreman's Terrace

D Boreman's "Steps"

E Greenwich castle

F The Keeper's Cottage

G One tree hill

H Le Notre's parterre

I The Queen's House

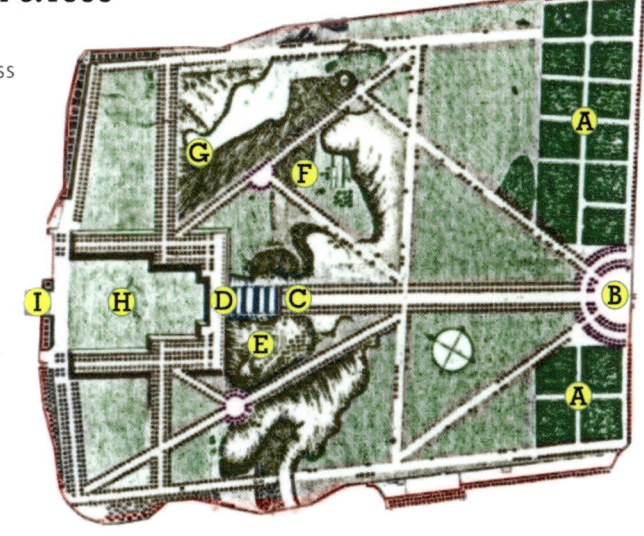

On the next pages a map shows the old layout of the park superimposed on the current layout. The similarities are remarkable with the south west quadrant being the most altered with the removal of the wilderness and one of the avenues that would transect the cricket pitch. Some drawings of the giant steps made after the construction of the observatory are also reproduced.
The small round building in the lower drawing on the right is Flamstead's well.

FACIES SPECULÆ SEPTEN:

From an old engraving. *Photo by Mr. Bouyer.*
ORIGINAL PORTION OF ROYAL OBSERVATORY, SHOWING FLIGHT OF STEPS.

PROSPECTUS ORIENTALIS.

GREENWICH PARK.
From an old print in possession of the Astronomer Royal.

Greenwich Park Map

Waterfront / North area:
- Cutty Sark
- Old Royal Naval College
- Market
- Nelson Rd
- Romney Rd
- Trafalgar Rd
- St. Alfege's Church
- Stockwell St
- King William Walk
- Nevada St
- Maritime Museum
- Queen's House
- Park Row

Gates:
- ST. MARY'S GATE
- PARK ROW GATE
- CREED PLACE GATE
- MAZE HILL HOUSE GATE
- MAZE HILL GATE
- VANBRUGH PARK GATE
- BLACKHEATH GATE
- CHESTERFIELD GATE
- CROOMS HILL GATE
- KING GEORGE STREET GATE
- CIRCUS GATE

Streets around the park:
- Crooms Hill
- Crooms Hill
- Rangers Vale
- General Wolfe Rd
- Chesterfield Walk
- Shooters Hill Rd (A2)
- Charlton Way
- Westcombe Park Rd
- Maze Hill
- Park Vista

Park features:
- Herbaceous Border
- The Queen's Orchard
- Boating Lake
- Playground
- Flower Garden
- Lake
- The Wilderness Deer Enclosure
- Bandstand
- Bower Avenue
- Great Cross Avenue
- Blackheath Avenue
- Cherry Tree Walk
- Tennis Courts
- Reservoir
- Rose Garden
- Cricket Pitch
- The Dell
- Tumuli
- Snow Hill
- King's Edge
- Conduit House
- The Avenue
- Jubilee Avenue
- The Parterre
- Herb Garden
- One Tree Hill
- Lovers' Walk
- Cross Avenue
- Giant Steps
- Observatory
- Queen Elizabeth's Oak
- Queen Elizabeth's Bower
- Pavilion Tea House
- Ranger's House

Compass: N, NE, E, SE, S, SW, W, NW

Over time, the great terraced steps that were to have been the cascade, have morphed into a bumpy slope with barely a trace of the terraces remaining. In 1790 the cobbled courtyard of the observatory was created by raising the land using gravel and constructing a retaining wall to hold it in place. A path was built in front of the observatory running alongside this wall and the meridian line was marked on it so you can step from the eastern to the western hemisphere as you cross it[32]. Excess building material from this work was dumped on the terraces further diminishing their stepped shape.

A survey in 1812 indicated that of the almost three thousand trees remaining in the park only twenty or so were still in a good state of health and growing. This resulted in a major replanting exercise over the next decade and a longer term maintenance plan was put in place because the trees were being killed by pollution as London became choked with the smoke and fumes from domestic coal fires and the factories of the industrial revolution.

The tall Scots pine trees that once elegantly framed the terraces were not suited to the soil or location, and had all been felled by the end of the nineteenth century. By 1915 all the avenues had been replanted with the original layout retained. In the 1970s, the remaining elm trees, which had formed such an important part of the original design, had succumbed to Dutch elm disease and been largely replaced by limes.

The much altered areas of coppice woodland installed by Boreman remain in their original location and these now form The Flower Gardens and The Wilderness, both providing a haven for wildlife, the deer and a creative outlet for the park gardeners [Map: K6].

Despite many changes, Greenwich Park remains an outstanding example of a four hundred year old French styled baroque landscape, with its avenues still following their original routes. For the majority of visitors this important historical fact goes largely unnoticed.

---

32 This path originally zigzagged down the hill on the west side towards the road and was paid for by Neville Maskelyne, the Astronomer Royal, following a bad fall one snowy winter. The Anarchist Bomb exploded on this path. It no longer exists.

The Park Wall

The wooden fencing installed by Humphrey, Duke of Gloucester, was replaced by a brick wall on the instructions of King James I. It was built between 1619 and 1625 for a cost of just over £2,000, the equivalent of around £400,000 today. The total length of the wall was 3.6 kilometres and on average it was 3 metres high and 300mm thick, requiring hundreds of thousands of bricks to complete it.

The fabric of the wall has been much modified over the years and the only original section is to be found by the Ranger's House. In the great storm of 1703 huge sections of the wall, some as long as five hundred metres (100 rods) were brought down[33]. New gates have been added and in some places the wall has been removed and replaced with iron railings to afford the surrounding houses a better view. In most other places the original wall has either collapsed and been replaced, or rebuilt as part of the wall of an adjoining building. The entire northern wall was moved and rebuilt in the nineteenth century.

The Northern Wall

Originally the Queen's House straddled the old Woolwich Road providing a bridge between the palace grounds and the park. For safety and privacy the road was bounded by high walls on either side roughly where the colonnades are today.

The southern wall of the road would have been the original northern wall of the park, but at the start of the nineteenth century the entire northern boundary of the park was moved about 15m south to provide additional grounds for Greenwich Hospital School which had recently occupied the buildings and was in the process of improving its facilities.

The wall in front of the Queen's House is referred to as the ha-ha and was erected in 1809 and remains largely unchanged from that time. A ha-ha is a combination of a ditch and low wall that can keep animals off lawns without

---

33 The City Remembrancer: Great Storm of 1703. Based on contemporary accounts this storm was a Category 2 hurricane.

obscuring the view. The ditch is now largely filled in as a herbaceous border. The central gate opposite the Queen's House gives an indication of the original structure of the ha-ha [Map: D4].

Image 46: The ha-ha gate. This is the only point where the sunken southerly side of the ha-ha can be seen, the rest having been filled in to make the herbaceous border.

Park Vista

Just through the gate at Park Row, the aptly named street on the right, Park Vista, has several buildings situated between it and the park. The largest is called The Chantry and was built around a small conduit house dating back to 1515. It became part of the Naval College school in 1807 and was significantly enlarged to provide accommodation for the auditor of the hospital [Map: D5].

The top of the original Tudor conduit house from the Palace of Placentia can be seen from the street and an impressive stone carving (presumably a nineteenth century reproduction) of the Royal Arms of Edward VI is visible where the modern exterior wall has been lowered. This wall would have been incorporated into the original northern boundary of the park making this building, at least in part, the oldest in Greenwich.

Image 47: Edward VI Coat of Arms on The Chantry in Park Vista

The oldest public house in Greenwich, The Plume of Feathers, can also be found on Park Vista. Built in 1691 and originally called The Prince of Wales, it would have not been so out of the way back then as Park Vista formed the main road from Woolwich to Greenwich.

St. Mary's Gate

Illustration 1: St Mary's gate

These attractive iron gates, painted black with elaborate gold detailing, were installed in 1929 to provide a new road entrance to the park from the centre of Greenwich [Map: D2].

There has been a gate in the north west of the park linking it to the centre of Greenwich since at least the time of Henry VIII. The modern road, The Avenue, used to run directly to the corner where a gate allowed access to and from Stockwell Street. Its position is identified by the gate house to the west of the current gates. The gate house is officially called St. Mary's Lodge and was constructed in 1808 when the northern wall was moved and served as park offices as well as providing accommodation for the gatekeeper. At that time the current St. Mary's gate was a row of iron railings.

The buildings that now line the south of Nevada Street did not exist then, the land being empty and used for temporary buildings during the Greenwich Fair. Permanent buildings were erected during the middle of the nineteenth century including the Rose and Crown music hall which is now the Greenwich Theatre, with a pub underneath it having taken its name.

Illustration 2: St Mary's Lodge, now a cafe.

St. Mary's Church (demolished)

The gates take their name from a church that no longer exists called St Mary's, which used to stand to the east of the current gate on land previously part of the park. The rectangular area containing a granite statue of William IV marks its former location. The church was a neoclassical design by George Basevi and Princess Sophia Matilda laid the foundation stone in 1823, it being completed a year later in 1824 [Map: D2].

During that time the centre of Greenwich was undergoing significant redevelopment and Greenwich Market, which had occupied the area east of King

William Walk since its charter was granted, was moved to the central position it occupies today.

St Mary's Church had been built to cater for overspill from St. Alfege's Church, but as the congregation declined it was closed and demolished in 1936 to provide better access to the new National Maritime Museum.

Image 48: St. Mary's Church PD

The Southern Wall

The southern wall remains in its original position as does Blackheath gate. This gate had always been one of the main entrances to the park as it linked the palace at Greenwich to the palace at Eltham.

During the first part of the great landscaping, the Blackheath gate was made a central feature of the design with the area around it being laid out as a semi-circular patte d'oie lined with chestnut trees four deep. It was known as The Round, but the construction of the police station and Keeper's Lodge in 1853 have altered this area permanently. Some of the original chestnuts remain and some new ones have been replanted on the western side where they would have stood.

Image 49: Park Lodge - Blackheath gate

In 1855 the wooden gates were replaced with new wrought iron ones, and these are the gates in place today, having been modified once or twice to accommodate modern traffic. Horses and carriages were allowed into the park from Blackheath in 1875 and the through route to St. Mary's gate was opened in 1887.

All Saints Church, Blackheath

Image 50: All Saints Church from Greenwich Park down Blackheath Avenue

Completing the symmetry of Blackheath Avenue in the distance can be seen the spire of All Saints Church in Blackheath which was built in 1858 on land provided by the Earl of Dartmouth. It is now a listed monument.

All Saints Church was the parish church of Terry Waite who, as a Church of England special envoy negotiating the release of hostages in Lebanon, was himself taken hostage in 1987. He was not released until 1991 and during this time a candle was kept burning in the church for him. Its bells were rung on the news of his release on 18th November that year.

The Strologo Shelter

Charles (Carlo) Dello Strologo was an Italian born in 1865 to a large wealthy family in Alexandria, Egypt, who had many interests including tobacco plantations. He married An Irish girl called Nellie in England in 1894 and retired with her to Surrey in 1933 where he bought a large farm house on Woodhill Lane, becoming a British Citizen in 1937.

In an act of rather unusual philanthropy he decided to provide a bus shelter for every village in his home county of Surrey and dedicate them to the king. This was reputedly because he felt sorry for the citizens of his adopted country having to wait for buses in such terrible weather.

The bus shelters are extremely sturdy being constructed from oak with cedar roof tiles. Having supplied the whole of Surrey he then provided shelters to the Royal Parks with Greenwich Park receiving theirs in 1938, the same year as his death [Map: K4].

Image 51: The Strologo Bus Shelter. The roof is made from cedar wood tiles.

Cornish Rebels

Following the imposition of taxation on tin mines to finance a war against Scotland, many areas of Cornwall suffered from extreme deprivation. The Cornish felt such a strong grievance against the English that Michael Joseph, a blacksmith, who was known as An Gof (Cornish for 'the Smith'), gathered 15,000 men and set off to London picking up support on the way as they marched through Salisbury and Winchester.

After a detour through Kent in a failed attempt to raise additional support, they made camp on Blackheath before intending to proceed to London Bridge. With all these diversions Henry VII had had ample time to prepare his army and on 17th June 1497 he launched a surprise attack while they were still on Blackheath in what became known as the battle of Deptford Bridge.

Most of the leaders were captured on the battlefield, but An Gof escaped and

Image 52: The Cornish rebellion plaque, in Cornish and English.

attempted to seek sanctuary in the Convent of the Observant Friars in Greenwich, but he was arrested before he could enter.

A plaque on the park wall outside Blackheath gate commemorates the leaders who were tried and executed at Tyburn ten days later. On his way to the gallows, An Gof requested that he be forever remembered by his fellow country men and this plaque honours his last wish in both English and Cornish [Map: L4].

Embrasures

Also outside and at the south west corner close to Chesterfield Walk are five small embrasures in the wall that would have provided defensive gunfire across Blackheath in the event of an invasion [Map: L3].

The high ground south of the Thames has always been considered to be extremely strategic because of its view over the river and London. This was even more so in 1940 when accurate artillery located here could have dominated any battle. For this reason places like these were very heavily defended and formed part of a ring of "stop lines" around London to halt an enemy invasion.

Image 53: Part of the wall facing Blackheath with two holes (embrasures) created during world war II to provide a defensive gun position.

The success of the Battle of Britain meant that an invasion never happened, but at The Point on Blackheath there is a memorial to an Australian Hurricane pilot called Richard Reynell who tragically lost his life there when his Hurricane was shot down on the first day of the blitz.

Greenwich War Memorial

Somewhat out of the way, the south east corner of the park wall has been removed and replaced by a circular space containing the official war memorial commemorating the lives of Greenwich residents who died while serving in the armed forces during the two world wars [Map: L7].

Figure 54: The Greenwich War Memorial

Made of Portland stone, it was unveiled on Armistice Day in 1922 by the father of local Victoria Cross recipient Cecil Sewell. It was updated after 1945 to remember those who fell in the Second World War.

The inscription reads:

> Borough of Greenwich in Glorious & Grateful memory of the men of this borough who gave their lives in the Great War. The number exceeds 1600 and their names are recorded in a roll of honour deposited in this memorial.
>
> Also in Grateful Remembrance of those residents of the Borough who gave their lives to the country during the war 1939-1945.

Nearby is a bandstand and the Vanbrugh gravel pit that once provided sand to spread on the kitchen floors of London, but is now partially filled in with rubble from buildings in the area bombed during the Second World War. Compared to the park, it is quite quiet, and is a small haven for wildlife, including birds.

Maze Hill Private Gates

At the lower end of Maze Hill, next to the playground, there is a row of five houses, numbered 32 to 40, which adjoin the park. Unusually each house has its own private gate into the park [Map: L3].

These were built between 1808 and 1812 on an old burial ground for Greenwich Naval Hospital which had become full and was closed in 1749, the bodies being moved to the grounds of Devonport House next to St. Mary's gate. Not all the bodies were moved though as the garden of No. 40 still contains the officer's mausoleum built in 1714 in red brick by Nicholas Hawksmoor. This is located at the southern end of the garden and its arched door and gable is visible on Maze Hill where it is incorporated into the wall.

These buildings originally formed an infirmary for sick children from the Royal Naval Hospital School (now the maritime museum), but by 1822 it had been converted into separate houses which were then let to hospital staff and eventually sold off as private homes. The officer's mausoleum was repaired and sealed at this time.

The Park during the World Wars

Most of the lower park, including the large flat area in front of the Queen's House that was to have been a Le Nôtre designed parterre, was allocated to allotments during the First and Second World Wars as part of the 'Dig for Victory' campaign. Although primarily a propaganda exercise designed to raise morale, it did contribute somewhat to the war effort by reducing the dependency on imported food.

Aerial photographs[34] reveal many outlines in this area including those of buildings, some of which would have been bomb shelters. There were three in Greenwich Park housing approximately five hundred people. One of these was underground in the Standard Reservoir (see Under the Park) which was even equipped with toilets, but another was excavated in 2020 on the parterre which has thick concrete walls just below the ground.

Image 55: Allotments in Greenwich Park PD (Unknown)

Anti-aircraft guns were placed in the south east corner of the park in the flower gardens. To give the guns a clear aim some of the older trees on the north side had their tops removed and this can still be seen in the winter when they are devoid of foliage.

---

34   The aerial images viewed with Google Earth / Maps show these markings.

Greenwich Castle

Image 56: A detail from Wyngaerde's sketch of 1558 showing the simple castle tower in the park behind the Palace of Placentia. In front of the palace note the arched bridge that provided access to the royal barges over the public right of way next to the river. PD

You might expect that the strategic high ground now occupied by the Royal Observatory should be home to a castle, and this was indeed once the case. It was built by Humphrey, Duke of Gloucester in 1437 and originally named Mirefleur after the castle mentioned in Amadis of Gaul, a heroic tale of chivalry written in the fourteenth century.

It is unlikely that this was the first fortified building on this commanding viewpoint and this conjecture is supported by the wording of the royal warrant which specifically states that the Duke was to construct the tower anew.

Humphrey's Mirefleur can be seen in a sketch of 1558 drawn by Wyngaerde prior to it being significantly enlarged. It appears to have been a well appointed but modest building, with a single buttressed tower surrounded by a moat and a window facing the river.

One of its first noted uses was when Mary of York, daughter of Edward IV, was sent up to the tower when she was sickly in the hope that the fresh air would be good for her. Unfortunately she died in the tower at the age of 14 in 1482.

Henry VIII made many alterations to Mirefleur during his reign including the creation of two new towers and the addition of some out-buildings. It remained fortified (crenelated) and now had a gatehouse before the moat. Looking much more substantial, the local population began to refer to it as Greenwich Castle. The old, more romantic, name of Mirefleur was still used at court even in the Elizabethan era.

Despite looking like a castle, it was primarily a hunting lodge and Henry VIII would have made good use of it as such. He found it useful for other things too. He stored wine and valuable items in the secure rooms and it also proved to be an ideal place to enjoy the company of at least one of his mistresses who he had take up residence there[35].

At the beginning of the seventeenth century, Henry Howard, Lord Northampton, wanted to live in the park so much that he purchased the rights to be Park Keeper. Henry Howard was a wealthy benefactor and founded the Trinity Hospital almshouse in Greenwich on the banks of the Thames which still provides a home for the old and in need today[36] [Map: A8]. He made the castle his primary residence, further enlarging it by adding conical turrets and other aesthetically pleasing features. It was surrounded by a wooden fence and its grounds were planted with various trees and shrubs.

Theophilus Howard, the Second Earl of Suffolk, became Park Keeper in 1616 and also spent much time in the castle, his wife, Elizabeth passing away there in 1633.

Image 57: Henry Howard in the Chapel of Trinity Hospital

35　The Arte of English Poesie, George Puttenham, 1589. Probably Elizabeth Blount, Henry's mistress for eight years and mother of his illegitimate son Henry Fitzroy.

36　Trinity Hospital, located next to the power station, was built in 1614, but was redesigned and rebuilt in 1812. It, therefore, predates the Naval College.

With its prominent position the castle was considered a place of military importance and by 1642 had been made a key part of the network of river defences along the Thames. In 1649, at the start of the Commonwealth, the soldiers stationed there were reported as being kept very busy preventing poachers 'liberating' deer from the park.

Perhaps the most unusual incident that the castle witnessed was the temporary incarceration of Robert Dudley, the Earl of Leicester in 1579. He had secretly married Lettice Knollys, Countess of Essex, but when this was discovered by Queen Elizabeth I it proved as embarrassing as it was distressing, since Dudley was well known as her consort.

'...whereat being not a little enraged, she confined him to the Castle of Greenwich, with purpose to have sent him to the Tower of London.'[37]

Fortunately for him, the Queen's initial fury abated, and instead of a one-way trip to the Tower, he was merely banned from court along with Elizabeth's cousin, Lettice.

GREENWICH CASTLE, 1637.

---

37 The Baronage of England, Sir William Dugdale

The Royal Observatory

Flamstead House

The first Astronomer Royal was Sir John Flamstead and the original building of the Royal Observatory is called Flamstead House to this day. A stone inscription over the original entrance door dated 1676 reads:

CAROLUS II REX OPTIMUS, ASTRONOMIAE ET NAUTICAE ARTIS
PATRONUS MAXIMUS SPECULAM HANC IN UTRI-USQUE
COMMODUM FECIT, ANNO DNI MDCLXXVI.
REGNI SUI XXVIII.
Curante Iona Moore, Milite R.T.S.G.

His Majesty King Charles II, Great Patron of the arts of astronomy and navigation commissioned this observatory for the benefit of both in the year of our lord 1676 and 28th year of his reign.

Image 58: Inscription on Flamstead House

By the care of Jonas Moore, Surveyor General of the Ordnance.

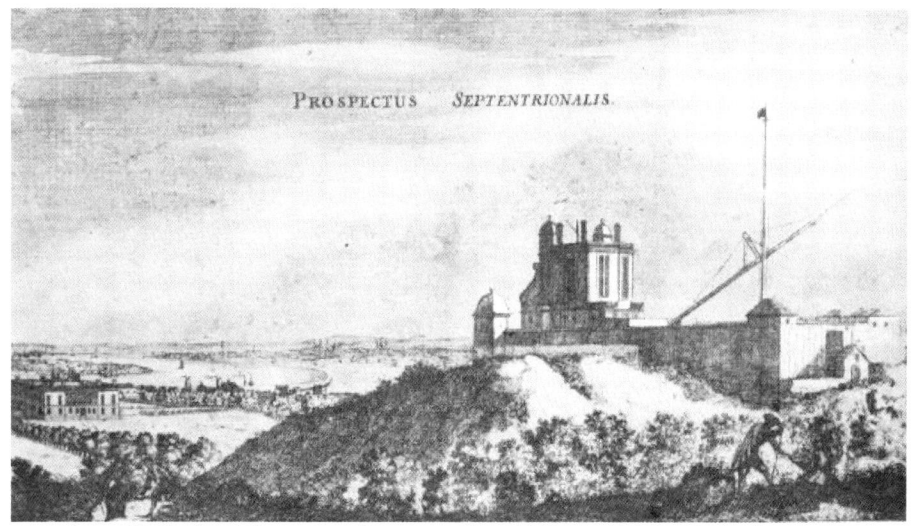

Image 59: The Royal Observatory after construction with Greenwich Palace in the distance. PD

Flamstead was born in Denby in Derbyshire in 1646 and was a weakly boy who lost his mother when he was only three. He took to reading and gained a place at the free school in Derby, but his consumption meant that he was too sick to attend university.

With help from his father he taught himself mathematics and astronomy and began to compile his own almanac recording the positions of the stars, thereby uncovering the poor quality of the currently published data. Rejected by the Royal Society, his work was noticed by Sir Jonas Moore of the Royal Ordnance who, in 1671, helped him construct his own observatory.

Sir Jonas Moore continued to mentor him helping him get a degree from Cambridge University before inviting him to work with him at the Tower of London.

In 1674 a French man named Le Sieur de St Pierre, who was known at court and had some influence, put forward a paper on measuring longitude. Such was the interest in accurate navigation at the time, that Charles II formed a Royal Commission to review the proposals. Sir Jonas Moore was a member of the commission as was Sir Christopher Wren, who was a professor of astronomy as well as an architect. The commission quickly dismissed the proposals as impractical as they had already been tried before, but one outcome was that through reading some of Flamstead's papers, Charles II became aware of the poor accuracy of the star tables used to aid navigation and decided to improve them.

John Flamstead was appointed the first Astronomer Royal and on the 22nd of June 1675 Charles II signed the warrant for Sir Jonas Moore to build an observatory in Greenwich Park on the site of the old castle to designs provided by Sir Christopher Wren.

Whereas, in order to the finding out of the longitude of places for perfecting navigation and astronomy, we have resolved to build a small observatory within our park at Greenwich, upon the highest ground, at or near the place where the castle stood, with lodging-rooms for our astronomical observator and assistant. Our will and pleasure is, that according to such plot and design as shall be given you by our trusty and well-beloved Sir Christopher Wren, Knight, our surveyor-general of the place and site of the said observatory, you cause the same to be fenced in, built and finished with all convenient speed, by such artificers and workmen as you shall appoint thereto, and that you give order unto our Treasurer of the Ordnance for the paying of such materials and workmen as shall be used and employed therein, out of such monies as shall come to your hands for old and decayed powder, which hath or shall be sold by our order of the 1st of January last, provided that the whole sum, so to be expended or paid, shall not exceed five hundred pounds; and our pleasure is, that all our officers and servants belonging to our said park be assisting to those that you shall appoint, for the doing thereof, and for so doing, this shall be to you, and to all others whom it may concern, a sufficient warrant.

Image 60: John Flamstead .PD

Image 61: The Astronomer Royal observing in the Octagonal Room. PD

The location was perfect, being on high ground and away from the smoky skies of the city. The ruins of Greenwich Castle were demolished, with the reusable timber, iron and lead retained to help economise, as the budget provided by the king was fairly meagre for such a significant project. Cheap but sturdy bricks were also salvaged from rebuilding work at Tilbury fort, where Elizabeth I had made her famous speech.

On the 10th of August of the same year, Flamstead attended the laying of the foundation stone of the new Royal Observatory. Designed by Sir Christopher Wren to incorporate the old castle's foundations and use the salvaged materials, the observatory was constructed In less than twelve months. Flamstead took residence on the 10th July 1676 and began his observations of the northern skies. Edmund Halley replaced him 42 years later and constructed an observatory on the island of Saint Helena[38] in the South Atlantic. Between them they mapped all the visible stars in the northern and southern hemispheres.

Flamstead House remains much as it was when first built, especially its front overlooking Greenwich and the Thames. An extension at the rear was added by Neville Maskelyne at the end of the eighteenth century and Halley had previously built the rooms on its eastern side which housed new and more accurate telescopes [Map: F4].

---

38   Saint Helena was the island where Napoleon Bonaparte was exiled.

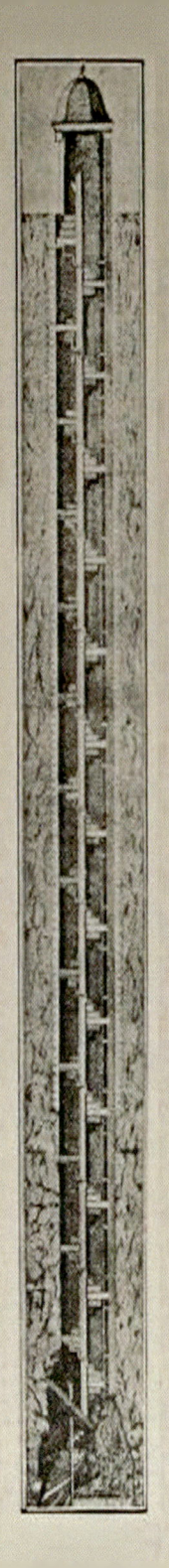

Flamstead's Well

A significant feature of the observatory that is no longer present is a well. This was not a well for the extraction of water although it may originally have been built for that purpose for Greenwich Castle. Rather, it was the location of a zenith telescope designed to observe stars directly overhead, the additional darkness of the well, and removal of all the surrounding light from the night sky, making observations more accurate.

This well was located in the expanded grounds of Flamstead House and was behind the new buildings that make up the south of the courtyard. Today there is a modern representation of a well close to the original site which was discovered following minor excavations in the area. When the observatory was first built it stood alone outside the building and can be seen in drawings of the time (see the earlier picture of the giant steps).

Flamstead did not end up making much use of the well for observations and this was attributed to the poor quality of the main lens which is still held at the Science Museum in London. Modern tests show that it would have provided very blurry images thereby negating all the advantages of being at the bottom of a dark and damp well.

Flamstead may well have been grateful for having a good excuse not to use the well, as spending hours in the confined and unpleasant space at the bottom with a slippery 35 metre climb to get out, would not have been the most inviting prospect for an evening.

Flamstead's Well PD

Prime Meridian

Image 62: The Royal Observatory and Meridian Line

In the courtyard of the Royal Observatory there is a brass strip running south to north embedded in the cobbles. This is the original Prime Meridian of 1884 and represents zero degrees longitude[39]. Standing astride it, you can picture yourself at the centre of the world, with one foot in the west and one foot in the east [Map: F4].

The aim of the Royal Observatory was to revolutionise navigation. When it was founded, ships could work out roughly where they were by carefully tracking their bearing and speed and occasionally fixing their position by using the stars in the night sky. It was already relatively simple to determine how far north you were from the equator because there was a fixed reference point in the sky called the Pole Star.

This star is aligned with the axis of rotation of the earth and so, unlike all the others, it does not appear to move. Once you find the Pole Star then you immediately know which direction is north. Measuring its angle from the horizon and using some simple mathematics you can then establish your latitude.

---

39 Because of the needs of modern technology, navigation today is based on a new standard introduced in 1984 called WGS84. For the best accuracy it was necessary to move zero degrees approximately 100 metres east of the Greenwich Meridian.

POLE STAR

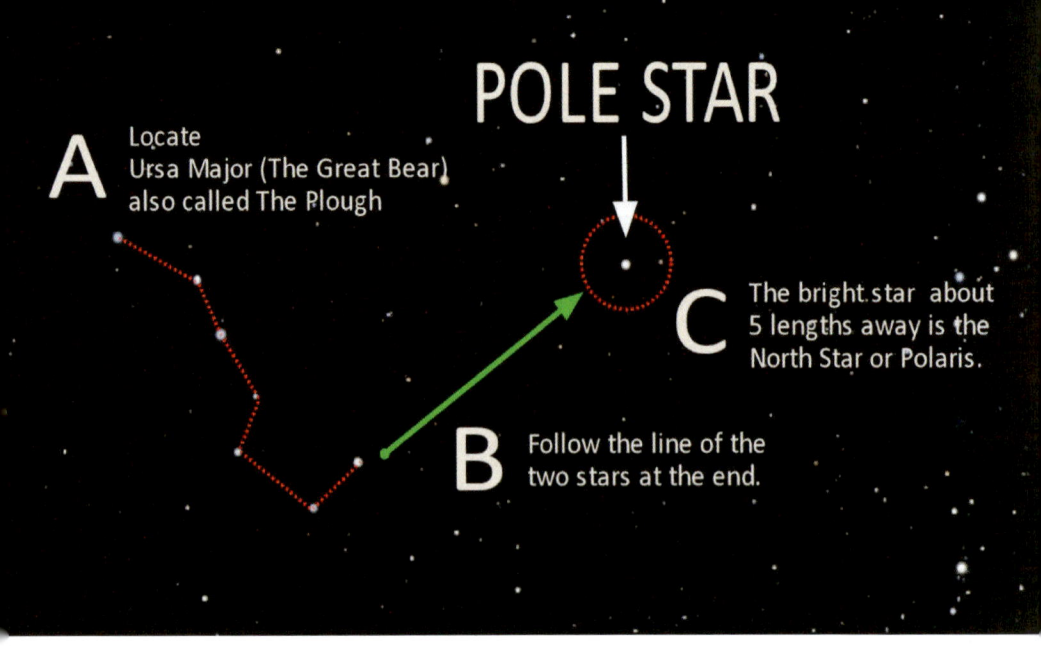

A Locate Ursa Major (The Great Bear) also called The Plough

B Follow the line of the two stars at the end.

C The bright star about 5 lengths away is the North Star or Polaris.

If you crossed the equator, then you could use a group of stars called the Southern Cross instead of the Pole Star.

Working out how far east or west you were is more challenging for three reasons. The first problem is that unlike latitude, longitude has no natural central point like the equator. In other words there is no concept of being in the east or west without creating an arbitrary line around the world, a prime meridian. The second problem was a lack of accurate star charts and the third, the need for an accurate clock.

The stars and sun do not move but appear to rise and set because the earth rotates beneath our feet, moving us. Imagine you are at the equator on a north-south line that you have decided is your prime meridian. You note the position of the brightest stars and then, by magic, instantly travel 1,650 kilometres to the west. One hour later the stars will all appear in the exact same positions in the sky as you noted at your meridian because the earth has rotated you back to where you had come from. This means that by matching the observed star positions to an accurate record made at your prime meridian at various times, you can work out the local time where you are.

If you had an accurate clock telling you the current time at your prime meridian you could then calculate how far round the Earth you were, or your longitude. In this example our local 'star' time would be one hour later than that shown on the clock, so we would know that we were 15 degrees west of our prime meridian. Such a clock did not exist.

The work of John Flamstead, and subsequently Edmond Halley, solved the second problem by producing accurate tables of star positions at the Royal Observatory. Since the use of these tables determined the position of a ship relative to the location of the telescope used to record them, and because the data from Greenwich was by far the best available, this meant that Greenwich became the de facto prime meridian of the world, solving the first problem too. This was eventually officially ratified by all countries in 1884 at a conference held in Washington DC in the United States.

At the start of the eighteenth century clocks were not just inaccurate, they also did not work on a ship. The best clocks were all based on the principle that a gently nudged weight swinging under gravity, a pendulum, maintained a constant rhythm that could be exploited by the clock to keep time. Perfect on dry land, the rolling motion of a ship rendered these pendulum based clocks useless because the ship's movement meant that it no longer had a constant rhythm. This required the invention of a completely new type of clock that could work at sea.

Keeping Time

This sea chronometer was developed by John Harrison over several years. He was born in Yorkshire in 1693 and was the son of a carpenter. He became fascinated with clocks from an early age and was manufacturing them by the time he was twenty. When the Longitude Act was passed in 1714 offering substantial financial rewards[40] to whoever could solve the problems of measuring longitude, Harrison rose to the challenge.

---

40 The rewards were around £10,000, well over one million pounds today.

He replaced the pendulum with a spring loaded oscillating flywheel which moved constantly independent of its orientation. This, in itself, solved the problem of telling the time at sea, but he also needed to significantly improve its accuracy. This was far more complicated and required many other innovations to compensate for temperature changes and the fact that the movement of a ship still had some impact on the mechanism.

Not only did he resolve all these issues, but by 1759 he had been able to miniaturise the clock such that it was only 130mm in diameter, and was therefore, easily carried. This, his fourth major version of the clock, was known as the "sea watch" or H4 and was such a masterpiece of engineering that it finally won him the Longitude Act prize.

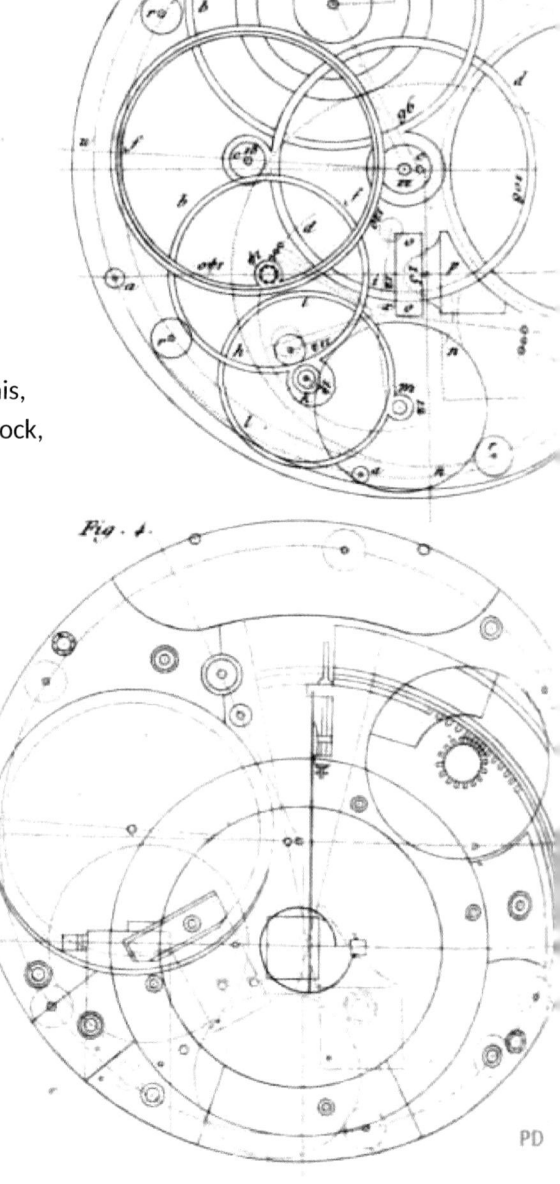

On the first test voyage in 1761 on HMS Dartford, H4 proved so accurate that after arriving in Jamaica after 81 days at sea it was shown to be just five seconds behind true time. The award panel initially refused to believe it could be that accurate and called for a second test. It required the personal intervention of King George III to ensure that Harrison received the prize money he so rightly deserved.

Equipped with an accurate clock, a clear sky, and tables of the Royal Observatory star data, ships could now tell where they were to within a mile or so, a major breakthrough in navigation.

Harrison's fascinating clocks can be seen in the Royal Observatory museum in the basement of Flamstead House. The link between astronomy, time and navigation had been firmly established at Greenwich and the Royal Observatory also became the time keeper of Britain.

The iconic red time ball on top of the observatory was installed much later, in 1833, to allow shipping moored on the Thames to set their chronographs accurately. The time ball is unusual because it is one of very few that still work. If you are in Greenwich Park just before one o'clock you can watch the red ball rise half-way up the mast, pause, and then continue to the top. At precisely one o'clock, irrespective of GMT or BST, it will fall.

The dropping of the ball would have been accompanied by the firing of a cannon, another technique used in harbours around the world to help shipping set the time. The visual signal provided by a time ball was considered superior to the firing of a cannon because there was no delay caused by the ignition process or the speed of sound, which itself would be influenced by the wind direction. However, bearing in mind the ultimate accuracy achieved from star readings, the ease with which the delay in sound could be compensated for, and the fact that in fog, the visual signal would have been useless, the time ball was really much more a show-piece than a revolution in timekeeping accuracy.

In 1852 the Shepherd Gate Clock was installed outside the observatory where it can still be seen today above some standard measures of length. It is an electric clock that keeps time through pulses sent by wires connected to a master clock within the main building. This master clock provided an extremely accurate time to a network of slave clocks set up around the observatory and also to other places around the Britain using telegraph wires so that clocks throughout the country could be synchronised.

The clock outside the observatory has a twenty four hour display and is accurate to within half a second. It shows Greenwich Mean Time throughout the year and so will appear one hour slow in the summer.

Image 63: The Shepherd Clock

The Greenwich Time Lady

In 1836 Henry Belville set up a business selling time. Each morning he would set his own chronometer at the Royal Observatory and then visit each of his two hundred subscribed clients so that they could set their clocks to the correct time. When he died, his wife continued to sell the time, and later his daughter, Ruth took on the role, becoming known as The Greenwich Time Lady.

Ruth became a minor celebrity in 1908 when a story about her appeared in The Times newspaper making disparaging comments about the old fashioned methods she was using which involved walking to her clients

Image 64: Ruth Belville getting the time from the Royal Observatory PD

with a chronometer she called Arnold. It also alluded to her using her feminine charm to keep her customers.

She suddenly found herself a focus of unwanted attention from reporters hoping for some form of scandal, but it soon emerged that the original story had been written by a rival setting up a business selling a service transmitting the time by telegraph. The old adage, 'No publicity is bad publicity' held true, and Ruth and Arnold continued to sell the time until she retired in the 1930s at over eighty years old.

From Navigation to Science

Once the stars were mapped and the time could be told accurately, the Royal Observatory could turn its attention away from matters of navigation and start exploring the workings of the solar system and universe. Sir George Biddell Airy became Astronomer Royal in 1835 and oversaw several major improvements to the observatory over the next 46 years.

He had the quirky Altazimuth Pavilion built in 1847 primarily to facilitate better observation of the moon and in 1850 installed the great transit circle[41] that now marks the position of the Prime Meridian. He also built The Great Equatorial Building which was completed in 1860 to house a much larger telescope for observing stars and the planets. This building originally had a cylindrical roof and looked a little like a water tower, but thirty years later this was replaced by the current astrographic dome.

Image 65: Astronomica carrying the sun and moon surrounded by the four signs of the zodiac. Designed by W.J.Neatby of Doulton & Co. Found on the north west side of the building.

The unusual, cross-shaped, South Building was built between 1891 and 1899 to allow the observatory to expand its scientific activities. It is constructed from red brick and terracotta giving it a very distinctive orange colour and it is covered in beautiful decorative features that tell the story of astronomy and include the names of twenty four historical figures from the observatory's past [Map: G4].

Horrox, 1619-1641, Astronomer. Predicted the transit of Venus in 1639
Wren.1632-1723, Astronomer, architect and founder of the Royal Society.
Flamsteed, 1646-1719, Astronomer Royal
Sharp, 1653-1742, Instrument maker and observatory assistant
Graham, 1673-1751, Instrument and clock maker
Halley, 1656-1742, Astronomer Royal

---

41 A transit circle is a telescope specifically for measuring star positions. It is mounted so that is can only rotate in the plane of the meridian and has a graduated circle attached allowing the elevation and time of star sightings to be recorded.

Bird, 1707-1776, Instrument maker
Dollond, 1706-1761, Lens and instrument maker
Bradley, 1693-1762, Astronomer Royal
Harrison, 1693-1776, Chronometer maker
Arnold, 1744-1799, Chronometer maker
Bliss, 1700-1764, Astronomer Royal
Earnshaw, 1749-1714, Chronometer maker
Herschel, 1738-1822, Astronomer
Maskelyne, 1732-1811, Astronomer Royal
Ramsden, 1735-1800, Instrument maker
Troughton, 1753-1835, Instrument maker
Pond, 1767-1836, Astronomer Royal
Simms, 1793-1860, Instrument maker
Baily, 1774-1844, Astronomer and founder member of the Royal Astronomical Society
Airy, 1801-1892, Astronomer Royal
Sheepshanks, 1794-1855, Astronomer & benefactor
Adams, 1819-1892, Joint discoverer of Neptune
Newton, 1642-1727, Astronomer and mathematician

Image 66: The first man in space, Russian, Yuri Gagarin. This statue is a replica of one in Russia traditionally visited by Russian cosmonauts before their first mission.

The industrial revolution had brought many foundries and other industry to Greenwich and the smoke and light pollution made London unsuitable for serious astronomy. The observatory was moved to Herstmonceux in Sussex in 1946, but even that location could not provide world-class observing conditions. Today the Royal Observatory is based in Cambridge and its 2.54m Isaac Newton telescope is at the summit of the Roque de los Muchachos on La Palma in the Canary Islands and controlled remotely.

In 1998 the Royal Observatory buildings became part of the National Maritime Museum and the most significant visitor attraction in the park.

The last building constructed on the site was the planetarium which opened in 2007 and is underneath the award winning 45 tonne truncated bronze cone with its attractive, ever changing patina. What is not obvious is that it is tilted at an angle of 51.5°, representing the latitude of Greenwich, and has a gully across the roof signifying the prime meridian. Finally there is a groove on the southern side that points directly to the Pole Star. The building won the annual Royal Institute of British Architects award in 2008.

At night a laser beam shines from the observatory and follows the line of the meridian. It was installed in 1993 and is located above the Transit Circle Telescope. The elevation angle had to be changed in 2017 because it was shining through the windows of some new flats in East London. It is visible 11 miles away at Chingford where an obelisk was built on the meridian line on the summit of Pole Hill by the Astronomer Royal in 1824 to assist in aligning his telescope.

Image 67: Pole Hill. The plaque on the obelisk reads: This pillar was erected in 1824 under the direction of the Reverend John Pond M.A. Astronomer Royal . It was placed on the Greenwich Meridian and its purpose was to indicate the direction of true north from the Transit Telescope of the Royal Observatory. The Greenwich Meridian as changed in 1850 & adopted by international agreement in 1884 as the line of zero longitude passes 19 feet east of this pillar,

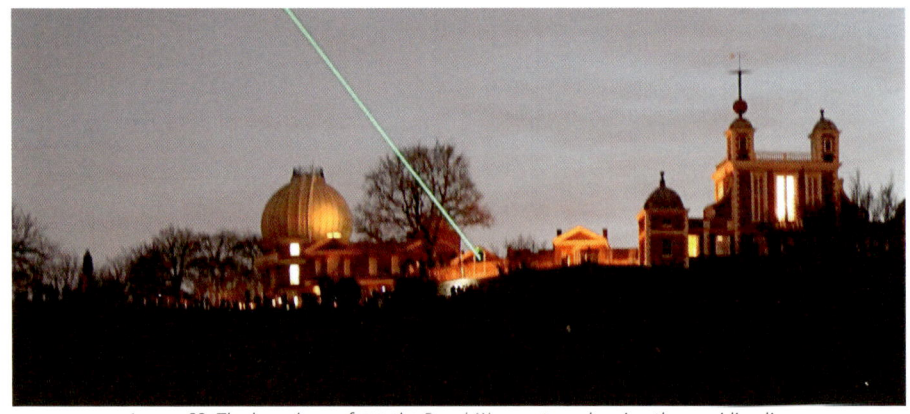

Image 68: The laser beam from the Royal Observatory showing the meridian line

Wolfe's Statue

Major General James Wolfe's statue has one of the best views in London [Map: G4].

It was unveiled on 5th June 1930 with many dignitaries in attendance and was a gift from the Canadian people. Wolfe, who was born in Westerham in Kent in 1727, had lived in Greenwich since he was eleven and always viewed Greenwich as his home.

The statue was created by Canadian Tait Mackenzie who has more than 200 other works spread around the world. A doctor by training, he used his knowledge of anatomy to create very life-like poses.

On the back of the plinth are shrapnel marks caused by a bomb dropped in the Second World War on 15th October 1940 that caused extensive damage to the observatory and its entrance gates, destroying the face of the original Shepherd Clock, which was replaced with a faithful replica.

The observatory was not a target, but was a landmark close to the river and so regularly flown over by the bombers on their way to London and the docks. As a result, many areas of South East London suffered from bomb blasts, often caused by bombers jettisoning any unused bombs before returning home. Greenwich Park had eleven bombs dropped on it during the blitz and was also damaged by one of the last V1 flying bombs ('Doodlebugs') in August 1944.

The Battle of Quebec or the Plains of Abraham

Wolfe led the English army to victory over the French at Quebec in 1759 claiming Canada as part of the British Empire. Britain had been at war with France since 1756 and it was viewed that attacking France in North America would be very profitable. The English laid siege to Quebec for three months making little progress as the French were firmly entrenched. Realising that he had to achieve a breakthrough, Wolfe launched a daring and difficult assault to capture the strategic high ground called the Plains of Abraham that overlooked the city to the west, thereby encircling the French garrison.

The French had placed very few soldiers protecting the side that faced the river as they deemed the 53m high cliffs there to be unscalable by an army. The English attacked stealthily at 4:00am on 13 September 1759 catching the French by surprise and quickly securing the summit. By 8:00am Wolfe had his entire force of 4,500 men lined up above the cliffs and ready to fight.

Not wishing to allow the English to dig in, the French counter attacked rather too hastily using the raw and amateur troops they had in position. They marched on

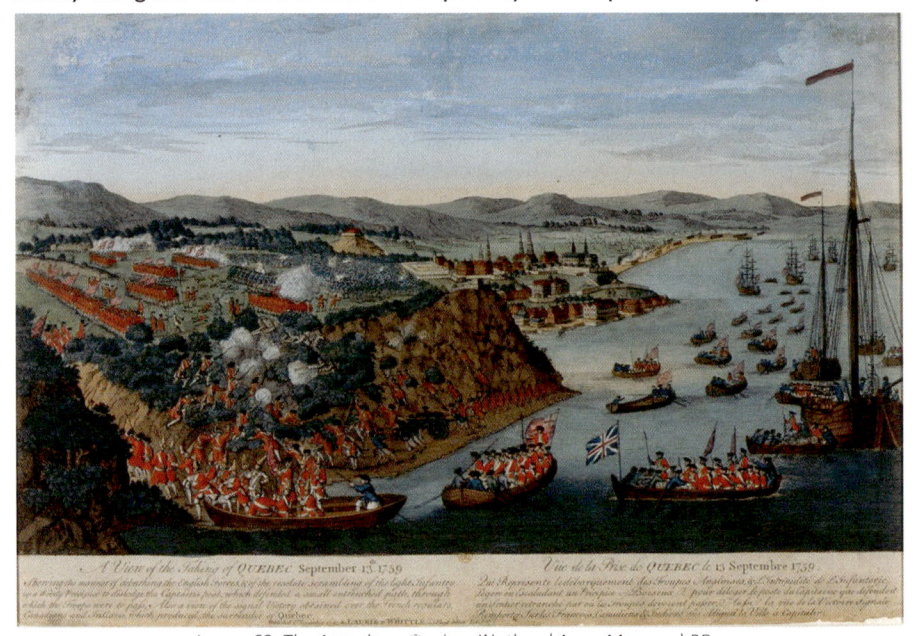

Image 69: The Assault on Quebec (National Army Museum) PD

the English line and began firing their guns as soon as they were in range, but the disciplined English held their nerve and delayed fire until the French were almost upon them at which point they unleashed a devastating rolling volley, forcing the French into a retreat from which they were unable to recover.

Tragically Wolfe was shot three times by musket fire during the initial assault and survived just long enough to learn that he had routed the French force and victory was his. Realising they could no longer hold Quebec, the remaining French garrison capitulated and left Canada.

Wolfe's body was brought back to England and lay in state in Macartney House, overlooking Greenwich Park, before being taken to St Alfege's Church where he was interred in the vaults.

His death was romantically captured by the Anglo-American painter, Benjamin West, and this painting is now in Canada. Another famous painting of his entitled 'The Preservation of St Paul after a Shipwreck at Malta' can be seen in the chapel of the Naval College, the only one of his works still in the place for which it was originally intended.

Image 70 The Death of General Wolfe, Benjamin West, 1770. PD

The Anarchist Bomb

On Thursday 15th of February 1894 at about 5:00pm, a loud explosion was heard all over Greenwich, and a cloud of smoke was seen rising above the trees next to the observatory. A park keeper, Patrick Sullivan, was the first to arrive on the scene and found a delirious young man kneeling in a pool of blood asking to be taken home in a distinctly foreign accent. The man was a twenty six year old French society tailor named Martial Bourdin, who had just blown himself up about halfway up the footpath[42] to the Royal Observatory.

He had lost his left hand and had several gaping wounds around his abdomen which were filled with metal shrapnel. He was rushed to hospital, but died from his injuries fifty minutes later, having been unable to talk or provide any explanation for what seemed to be a dreadful and inexplicable accident [Map: F3].

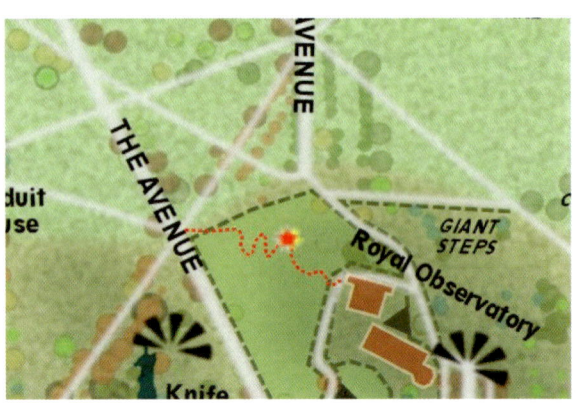

Image 71: Location of the explosion

His pockets contained some papers on how to manufacture explosives and a membership card to the Autonomie Club, a club at 6 Windmill Street in Fitzrovia, known for being frequented by radicals and anarchists. He was also in possession of £13, the equivalent of almost £2,000 today.

The next day police struggled to keep crowds of sightseers away from the crime scene. Inspection of the device revealed it was based on picric acid and triggered by sulphuric acid, a very dangerous and unstable combination of materials, explaining the accident. A search of his home and his brother's tailor shop, revealed nothing of any significance.

---

42 This path no longer exists. It would have zig-zagged down the hill from the east side of the observatory to the foot of the escarpment.

Image 72: Picture from the London Illustrated News showing the scene of the crime marked with a white cross. PD

Witnesses reported seeing him with another man in Westminster before boarding a tram to Greenwich where he was observed entering the park though St. Mary's gate wearing an overcoat with a brown felt hat and carrying a parcel. It seemed that he had possibly stumbled and fallen to the ground setting off the bomb that he was carrying.

Anarchist attacks in London and across Europe at the end of the nineteenth century had become relatively common and often targeted high profile government locations for publicity, so the observatory might well have been the target as it represented the empire and the establishment. With no apparent reason for him to be where he was unless the observatory was the target, this is what the police concluded. The money was presumed to be to fund his escape to France, or even America, where he had previously lived.

What exactly Bourdin was intending to do remains a mystery to this day, but such was the interest in this crime and its motivation, that it inspired several writings, including the novel The Secret Agent by Joseph Conrad. There were many conspiracy theories put forward, including the one that Conrad exploited in his novel, where it was supposed that Bourdin had been tricked into carrying out the bombing by a government agent who wanted to discredit anarchist movements.

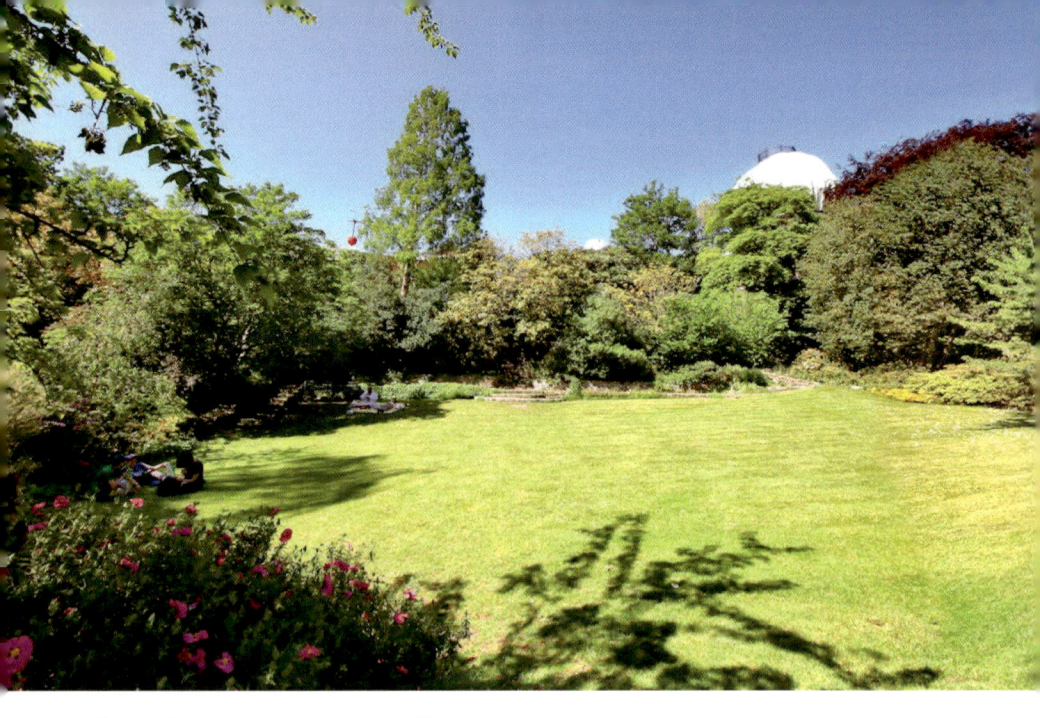

The Observatory Garden

To the west, and beneath the observatory, is a small secluded garden. It was once a quarry for excavating gravel and this accounts for it being a steep-sided, sheltered and shady location with its own pleasant microclimate. It is accessed from a path that passes in front of the observatory and takes you over some brass plates marking the position of the prime meridian. The gates to the garden are on the left, just before the path reaches the road through the park [Map: G3].

It was once the private garden for the Astronomer Royal, and he and his family could access it from the basement of Flamstead House through a gate. The area was returned to the park when the Royal Observatory moved to Herstmonceux. You can climb up and walk through the paths between the flower beds at the back of the garden to find the original entrance from Flamstead House.

The present entrance was built in the 1960's and local residents often refer to it as the 'Secret Garden', presumably because it is so well hidden and rarely visited, despite being in the centre of the park. On a nice day it is a lovely spot for a picnic and it even has picnic benches.

Ice House and Snow Well

In 1619, James I had an ice house built in the park. Ice houses were designed to store snow and ice collected in the winter, and keep it from melting, so that it could be used to cool drinks during the heat of the summer. They became common on the estates of the wealthy, but this one in the park was probably the first modern ice house in England.

Ice houses were placed in a cool and shady north facing position that was close to an area where snow and ice would form, typically a lake, pond or somewhere that flooded. When the ice house was built, the Observatory Garden was still an old sand and gravel quarry, and would have naturally collected snow and ice.

The building would have consisted of a brick lined hole, probably covered by a thatched roof to provide the best insulation. The ice house and well were probably demolished and filled in during the restoration of the park and observatory in the mid-nineteenth century[43].

---

43 Its location is unknown, but it could have been in the Observatory Garden or adjacent to it on the hillside next to the path that runs around Flamstead House.

The steep road coming up from St Mary's gate is called Snow Hill, and it is also known that a well existed opposite the Observatory Garden on the other side of the road. Referred to as the Snow Well (See Under the Park), this was nine metres deep and connected by a conduit to the stockwell that provided water to the public in Greenwich.

Image 73: The Greenwich Ice House, Samuel Hieronymous Grimm, 1772 PD

The only known picture of the ice house is by Samuel Grimm who was renowned for his detailed drawings. This would place the ice house at roughly the same location as the Snow Well and it could be that the building served a dual purpose as both a well and conduit house.

It may simply be that the drawing is mislabelled and is not the snow well at all. It looks remarkably similar to an existing Tudor conduit house in Eltham that served the royal palace there.

Image 74: The Tudor conduit house in Eltham (OS Ref: TQ436742)

Magnetic Observatory

The Royal Observatory once had a small outpost within the park where they could take measurements of the Earth's magnetic field. This was located in a square plot of land, just to the north of the flower garden and at the end of Great Cross Avenue.

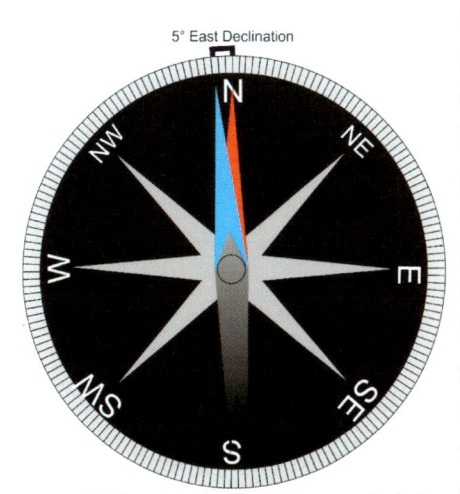

Image 75: Compass showing how magnetic declination affects accuracy. The red needle is pointing to magnetic north, but with 5 degrees east of declination the actual true north is shown by the blue needle.

The magnetic north pole is not fixed and moves around. In fact, there is evidence that in the past the north and south poles have flipped completely and changed position. To be able to navigate accurately with a compass it is, therefore, important to know the magnetic declination. This value gives the degrees difference between the actual north pole (used by the map) and the magnetic north pole (shown by the compass). In 2020 it was 5° east and it is currently increasing by about 1° every five years.

In 1816 the Admiralty requested that the Royal Observatory measure the declination accurately and John Pond, the Astronomer Royal at the time, built a housing for the equipment on the slopes of the Observatory Garden. Unfortunately, since the escarpment is made of sand and gravel, this began to subside and had to be abandoned. After several years of discussion, by which time George Airy had become Astronomer Royal, a new site was agreed where the Planetarium dome now stands. A wooden building was erected in 1839 and included a 25m high mast to improve measurement accuracy.

This was used until 1894 when the addition of the Altazimuth Pavilion and the Great Equatorial Telescope meant that the level of magnetic interference from all the new equipment in such close proximity was far too high to get accurate readings.

A new site, far from any magnetic interference was selected in the east of the park. The Christie enclosure was fenced off in 1897 and the new Magnetic Pavilion was completed in 1898 with all the equipment moved across and several peripheral buildings added [Map: H6].

Image 76: The Magnetic Pavilion in the Christie Enclosure. The small building housed meteorological instruments. PD

The arrival of the railway and the introduction of trams on the Woolwich road had some impact on the accuracy of the readings, but these were not significant. However, the electrification of the railway would have caused too much interference, so before this took place in 1926, the Magnetic Pavilion was moved to Leith Hill in Surrey.

The Christie Enclosure remained in place for another 30 years with the buildings being used for storage and meteorological observations. It was eventually demolished in 1959 and the parkland returned to its former state. There is no visible trace of these buildings today.

Image 77: Location of the Magnetic Observatory

Views

There are fine views over Greenwich and London from almost anywhere on the top of the escarpment, each location revealing something new.

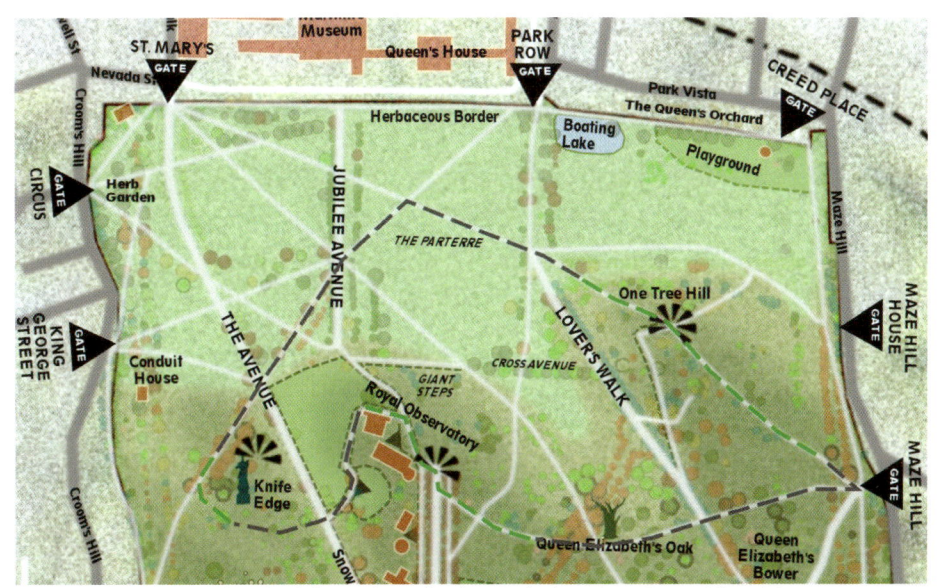

Image 78: A short but hilly circular walk taking in the best views Greenwich Park has to offer. The green dashes are where the most expansive views can be found.

View from the Royal Observatory

This is by far the most popular view in the park because of its proximity to the observatory [Map: G4]. It is also the best view of historical Greenwich where you can see the Queen's House, Old Royal Naval College and Cutty Sark most clearly. In the background, with the Thames wrapping itself around either side, is the Canary Wharf financial district. To the left are the eclectic buildings of the City of London and to the right, the dome of the O2 entertainment centre.

The large viewing space by the statue of General Wolfe can get extremely crowded at peak times, so to enjoy the view in a more relaxed and reflective fashion you should visit early in the morning, or even in the early evening, when the morning or evening sun can make the landscape even more striking.

The view from the observatory in 1989 (above) and 2019 (below).

Views at night.

View from One Tree Hill

One Tree Hill is one of the main viewpoints in the park and so called because it has one large tree on its summit. This tree, with a seat around it, is a London plane and is a replacement for one that was blown down in a storm in 1848 [Map: F5].

The panorama here is framed between arguably the best views of the observatory and Vanbrugh Castle. It stretches from the London-Eye at Westminster, past the Shard at London Bridge, then Saint Paul's Cathedral and the City of London before reaching Canary Wharf. A stroll towards the Maze Hill gate provides plenty more variations of the view including one that looks over the eastern stretch of the Thames.

Image 79: The observatory from One Tree Hill

One Tree Hill was originally known as Sand Hill. Before it was paved at the top, it had several trees, and the acid grass was so thin that the ground revealed the loose gravel and sand that makes up the ridge of the escarpment. In old drawings of the park it can be seen that it was even quarried on the western side.

The long wooden seat against the low wall behind the tree has an inscription which is the fifth verse of a poem that bemoans the fact that a place as lovely as One Tree Hill has no great poem written about it[44].

---

44   Originally published in The London Chronicle, May 25th-27th 1784, full prose from "The Weekly Entertainer" July 19th 1784.

London from Greenwich Park, 1809, JMW Turner (Painted on One Tree Hill) PD

One Tree Hill with its London Plane and the view of London (2021)

An Ode to One Tree Hill

To Cooper's Hill, so green and gay,
How sweetly Denham tun'd the lay!
Of Gronger's height soft Dyer sung;
And Richmond wak'd the lyre of Young:
Each flow'ry hill that charms around,
A poet's grateful praise has found,
Save one, that claims the muse's skill,
The pride of Greenwich, One Tree Hill.

Tamesis, chief of rivers, say,
In all thy wand'ring, winding way,
Doft thou so fair a hill remark
As this, the pride of Greenwich Park?
I know thou'lt say, and answer true,
"Not such a beauty meets my view."
Go, Richmond, fam'd for prospects still,
And bow thine head to One tree Hill

Italia's sons their Hybla boast,
The fairest hill on Sic'ly coast;
With all its charms, the peasant knows
How fierce the burning Syroc blows;
Such languor spreading with its breath,
As leads to sickness, oft to death:
Here no such terror comes to kill –
Health's blest retreat is One Tree Hill.

O how thy college, through the green,
Old Greenwich, dignifies the scene!
Nor that alone – it fills the breath
With rapture, scarce to be express'd;
Soft rapture! Rais'd to pearl the eye,
From Britain's bless'd philanthropy!
Ye vet'rans tars, here wander still,
And rest your limbs on One Tree Hill.

Here fair Eliza, virgin queen
From bus'ness free, enjoy'd the scene
Here oft in pensive form she stood
And kindly plan'd for Britain's good:
So record tells and this beside,
Sung ditties to the silver tide
Full worth such honours art thou still
Belov'd of thousands, One Tree Hill.

O here, how sweet, while nature's gay,
To mark the river's wreathy way;
There white wing'd commerce daily pours
The riches of a thousand shores;
Whilst bright Augusta, in return,
Deals matchless treasures from her urn:
Not though, fam'd Windsor, royal still,
Can shew such scenes as One Tree Hill.

Here let me at the early hour,
Beneath this tree enjoy the show'r
That when the fleeting cloud's gone by,
The rainbow's tints may glad mine eye;
The while the song-birds warble sweet,
In coverts green, below my feet;
Coverts yielding many a rill,
That whisper soft to One Tree Hill.

Here let me oft, at sultry noon,
When roses fill the lap of June,
Inhale the breeze that sweeps the glade
Where nature's fairest carpet's laid,
And the wild thyme, offering free
Its lips to cheer the roving bee;
At this warm hour, when all is still,
Here let me breathe on One Tree Hill.

Here oft the rising wave survey,
Illumin'd by the beams of day,
Yon crested herds, the nimble doe
That trips the fairy lands below;
And thou, of cities sure the queen,
Whose argent turrets close the scene,
Renown'd Augusta, who can'st fill
The minds with bliss from One Tree Hill.

Here often let me stray awhile,
And, Poplar, view thy verdant isle,
Whose pastures rear a finer fleece
Than any in the isles of Greece;
Then as from charm to charm I rove,
O Kent! I'll sing the land I love,
Where ev'ry scene delights me still,
But none, ye swains, like One Tree Hill.

Figure 80: One Tree Hill from the air in 1845 courtesy of Jules Arnout the French balloonist
Note the poor condition of the tree, the deer and 'Fame' behind the Queen's House. PD

Vanbrugh Castle

To the east of One Tree Hill, across the escarpment, the turrets of a castle can be seen. These belong to Vanbrugh Castle, a building maintained by the Blackheath Preservation Trust and converted to luxury flats which are leased to residents [Map: G7].

It was built by Sir John Vanbrugh between 1718 and 1726, supposedly in the likeness of the Bastille Prison in Paris where, as a young man, he had spent the last few months of a four year imprisonment having been found guilty of spying charges[45]. It was an unusual design for the time, evoking medieval styling and predating the Gothic revival that occurred thirty years later.

---

45   He was working undercover in Europe helping to orchestrate the invasion of Britain by William of Orange to depose James II and impose parliamentary rule.

Vanbrugh had become the Surveyor of the Royal Naval Hospital in 1716 when he was 52 and he lived in Vanbrugh Castle from 1719 to 1726, during which time he was continually enlarging and altering the building to accommodate his family and relatives. It does share several outward similarities to the old Greenwich Castle which had been demolished in 1675 to make way for the observatory and it would be nice to think that he was influenced, at least in a small part, by a desire to recreate it.

Prior to arriving in Greenwich, he had combined two very different careers. As a pre-eminent architect he was responsible for designing some of Britain's most famous and impressive stately homes, notably Blenheim Palace and Castle Howard. As a dramatist he wrote restoration comedies such as 'The Provoked Wife'. He had even managed to combine these activities by designing and building the Haymarket Theatre in central London.

Image 81: Vanbrugh Castle on Maze Hill from One Tree Hill at sunset.

The View from Knife Edge

The trees on the western escarpment restrict what can be seen from this point [Map: G3], but moving around opens up the views, including the one above showing the lime trees lining The Avenue with the Old Royal Naval College and Canary Wharf as the backdrop. You also get a different perspective on the Royal Observatory from here and a good view of the spire of Our Ladye Star of the Sea Church.

Large Standing Figure: Knife Edge

There are few notable works of art in Greenwich Park and so it is good to know that Henry Moore personally selected this location for his statue when it was installed in 1979. Cast in bronze at the famous Hermann Noack foundry in Berlin, it was removed in 2007 by its owner, the Henry Moore Foundation, because of concerns over graffiti and a spate of thefts of bronze statues which were being melted down for scrap metal. It was reinstated in time for the 2012 Olympics.

Large Standing Figure: Knife Edge was finished in 1976 and is one of several statues called Knife Edge. The sculpture is sometimes also called Winged Figure or Standing Figure (Bone) since it is based on a fragment of a bird's breastbone. The characteristic sharp diagonal detailing of the bone has been supplemented by a base and a rounded head to create a composition that resembles a human torso and evokes comparison to classical Greek sculptures [Map: G3].

Henry Moore is a key figure in British art and one of the world's best known abstract sculptors with prominent examples of his work around the world in almost every major city. This sculpture is very typical of Henry Moore's style, but he also had a passion for exhibiting his works in open space: "Sculpture is an art of the open air. I would rather have a piece of my sculpture put in a landscape, almost any landscape, than in, or on, the most beautiful building I know."

Moore's career was heavily influenced by war. He began work as a teacher, but after surviving a gas attack at the battle of Cambrai in the First World War, he moved into art using his ex-serviceman's grant. During the Second World War he was an official war artist and during this time established a strong reputation, culminating in a retrospective of his work at the New York Museum of Modern Art in 1946.

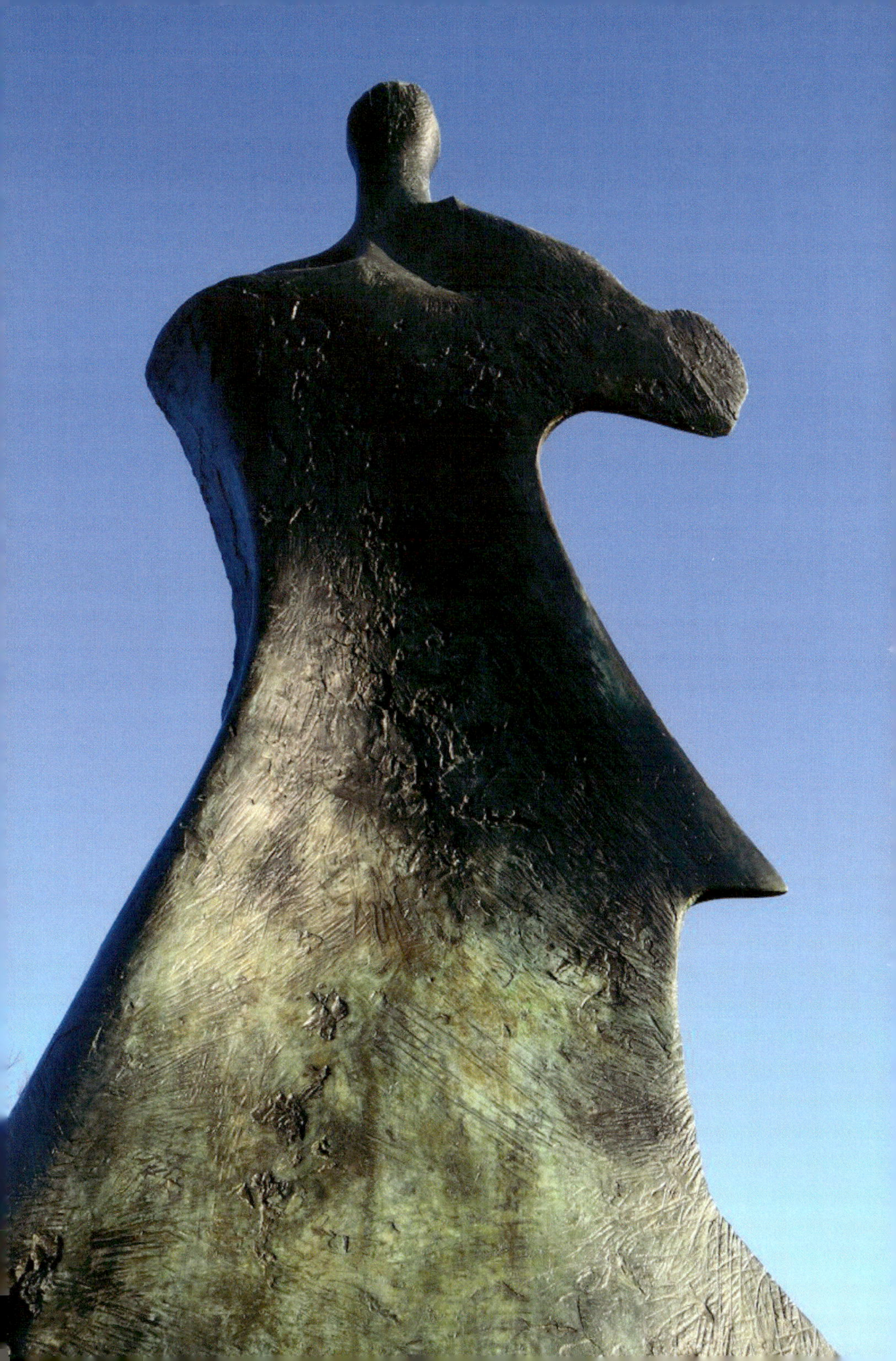

Our Ladye Star of the Sea Church

Also clearly seen from this viewpoint is the striking landmark spire of Our Ladye Star of the Sea Church [Map: F1].

It was originally established in 1793 as a small chapel to serve the significant number of Catholic seamen in the Royal Naval Hospital and was located on Park Vista in the garden of the architect, James Taylor.

This soon proved to be too small, and this new church in classic Victorian Gothic style was built between 1846 and 1851. Funding was organised by the North family who donated the land on Croom's Hill and received significant donations from the congregation and The navy. The two North brothers, who were both catholic priests, are buried in the church within a marble tomb.

Image 82: Our Ladye Star of the Sea Church

The interior of the church was designed by Augustus Pugin who was a famous architect responsible for many notable gothic buildings of the time, including the Tower of Westminster, or 'Big Ben' as it is often incorrectly called. Pugin was also a strong influence on William Wardell, the overall designer of the building, whose high altar was considered to be of such artistic merit that it was put on show at the Great Exhibition of 1851 before being installed[46].

---

46 Historic England Ref:1358941

Park Keeper

Prior to the creation of the role of Park Ranger, Park Keepers were appointed, who were responsible for ensuring that the parkland and its infrastructure were managed and kept in good shape for use by the sovereign.

Keeper of a Royal Park was a prestigious role and gave the holder considerable status and privileges within the court. Although there was some payment from the Crown, this was relatively insignificant. When the palace at Greenwich fell out of favour, the role of Park Keeper could be bought, and so the later Park Keepers were effectively leasing the park, the cottage and the castle so that they could live there.

The father of James I (originally James IV of Scotland), Henry Stuart Lord Darnley, was Park Keeper and perhaps explains the interest of James I in the park when he became king.

The most notable Park Keeper was Henry Howard, Lord Northampton, who bought the right to the title from Robert Cecil in 1605 who had been given the role for life, but did not want it. At the same time Henry Howard also leased the palace of Old Court so that he had somewhere to live. He already owned land in Greenwich and had a strong attachment to the area since it was where he had been brought up. In fact he had actually spent much of his childhood living in Greenwich Castle with his Aunt, Mary FitzRoy[47], so it was not too surprising that he spent £2,000[48] redeveloping Greenwich Castle into his home.

He was well respected by James I, but he did not get on well with Queen Anne, whom he upset on numerous occasions by speaking his mind. When Robert Cecil died, Henry Howard had hoped he would retain the right to be Park Keeper, but James I gave the park and all its properties to Anne. Much angered, he was forced to leave Greenwich despite his substantial investment and emotional ties and retire to his estate in Northampton. The castle reverted to his family after he died.

---

47 Lady Mary Howard who married Henry VIII's illegitimate son Henry Fitzroy.
48 Equivalent to c.£650,000 today.

List of Keepers of Greenwich park

1486 George Keene (Henry VII)
1517 Sir Nicholas Carew, courtier (Henry VIII)
1519 Sir William Compton, courtier (Henry VIII)
1527 William Carey, courtier (Henry VIII)
1528 William Norreys, courtier (Henry VIII)
1531 Sir Henry Norreys[49], courtier (Henry VIII)
1538 Sir Thomas Speke, courtier (Henry VIII)
1539 Sir Richard Long, courtier (Henry VIII)
1547 Henry Stuart Lord Darnley, father of James I (Henry VIII)
1550 Nicholas Dowsing, Keeper of the House of Greenwich (Henry VIII)
1553 Sir Henry Jerningham, Vice Chamberlain (Mary I)
1572 Sir George Howard, Master of Ordnance (Elizabeth I)
1580 Sir Christopher Hatton, Lord Chancellor (Elizabeth I)
1594 Thomas Sackville, First Earl of Dorset, Privy Councillor (Elizabeth I)
1605 Robert Cecil, Viscount Cranbourne. Lord high Treasurer (James I)
1605 Henry Howard, Earl of Northampton (Bought title from Robert Cecil)
1611 Thomas Howard, Earl of Suffolk, Lord Chamberlain (James I)
1614 Edward Somerset, Earl of Worcester, Privy Councillor (James I)
1616 Theophilus Howard, Lord Howard de Walden (James I)
1633 Henry Rich, Earl of Holland (Charles I)
1634 Uriah Babington, Keeper of the King's Gardens (Charles I)
1650 Sir Henry Mildmay (Commonwealth)
1662 Earl of St. Albans (Charles II)

The Keeper's Cottage

Directly south east of Queen Elizabeth's Oak, a Keeper's Cottage was once situated. It is mentioned in documents regarding the sale of the park proposed by Oliver Cromwell's puritans which dates it to before the mid-seventeenth century. Its exact date of construction is unknown, but Henry Howard was most likely responsible [Map: G5].

Although it is called the Keeper's Cottage, it was a functional set of buildings and unsuited for the official Keeper. It was almost certainly where the actual Keeper of the park lived and where they, and their family, spent their days looking after the grounds, trees and deer.

---

49 Executed for having an adulterous relationship with Anne Boleyn

It was surrounded by a private area of parkland that was walled or fenced off. This contained an orchard as well as the ancient Queen Elizabeth's Oak, or Old Oak as it would have been known. The cottage was a substantial building with several outbuildings and its own large iron water pump outside at the back. It was demolished in 1853 and the Keeper's Lodge by the Blackheath gate was built to replace it. There is also a stone trough near here that would have been within the grounds to provide water for any animals owned by the keeper.

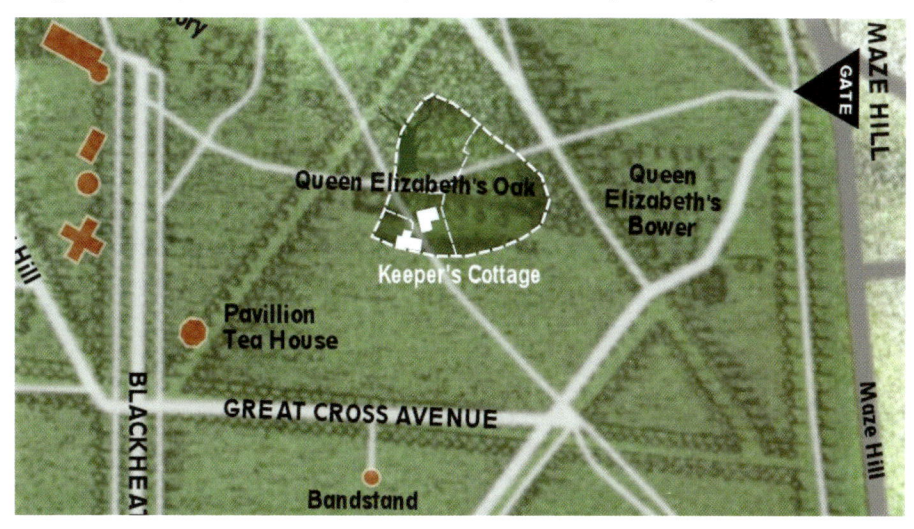

Park Ranger

List of Park Rangers

1690 Charles Sackville, Sixth Earl of Dorset & Middlesex
1697 Henry Sydney, Earl of Romney[50]
1707 Prince George of Denmark (Consort to Queen Anne)
1709 Henry Aylmer, Lord Aylmer, Master of the Horse[51]
1720 Sir John Jennings, Governor of Greenwich Hospital
1743 Lady Catherine Pelham
1805 Queen Caroline of Brunswick (Princess of Wales)
1814 Duke of Clarence (later King William IV)
1816 Princess Sophia Matilda of Gloucester, niece of William III
1844 George Hamilton-Gordon, 4th Earl of Aberdeen
1860 Lord Canning
1862 Prince Arthur of Connaught, the third son of Queen Victoria.
1877 The Countess of Mayo
1888 Field-Marshal Lord Garnet Wolseley
1896 Role of Ranger of Greenwich Park abolished by Parliament.

The Queen's House becomes the Ranger's Lodge

William III introduced the new sinecure title[52] of Ranger of Greenwich Park in 1690 and made the Queen's House the 'Grace and Favour' property associated with the title as it had been lying empty for some time. He appointed Charles Sackville as the Park Ranger whom he had brought back to court as the Lord Chamberlain.

Charles Sackville had been a great friend of Charles II and, as part of the infamous 'Merry Gang', was renowned for his ready wit, notorious womanising, disreputable behaviour and profligacy. It was Charles Sackville who had introduced Charles II to his most famous mistress, Nell Gwyn. His talents did not

---

50 Diverted the road from Woolwich to Deptford to run between the Queen's House and Greenwich Palace. Part of the road is called Romney Road after him.
51 The Master of the Horse was a ministerial role responsible for the king's horses and hounds.
52 A title having no official responsibilities.

make him popular with the strongly Catholic James II, but he was restored to favour when William III took the throne.

The Earl of Romney bought the title in 1697[53] and carried out many repairs, taking advantage of the creation of the Naval Hospital to also move the old Woolwich road that ran under the Queen's House to its current position where it became known as the Romney Road.

From 1709 the Naval Hospital petitioned parliament to allow the governor of the hospital to live in the Queen's House and so, in 1720, he was made Park Ranger. However, it proved far too costly to maintain the building and the decision was taken to provide accommodation for the governor in the hospital itself and returned the Queen's House to Caroline of Ansbach, Queen to George II, in 1730.

In 1743 Lady Catherine Pelham, wife of the Prime Minister, Henry Pelham, became Ranger of Greenwich Park and she and her husband moved into the Queen's House. Lady Pelham took an active role in restoring the much neglected park, even prosecuting a member of her staff that had clandestinely cut down some trees and sold them. After she died in 1780 the title of Park Ranger remained unoccupied for several years.

When Princess Caroline of Brunswick was greeted at the Queen's House in 1795 on her way to marry the Prince of Wales, she may have already thought about it as her potential home as it had been for so many English queens before her. She did eventually become Ranger in 1805, but by then she had separated from the prince and was living happily in Montagu House on Blackheath which also adjoined the park.

On 3rd October 1806 the Naval Hospital, which was running out of space and wanted to expand its school, agreed to buy the rather run-down Queen's House from the Crown. George III asked parliament to arrange for the Queen's House to be sold and, on 25th April 1807, the Queen's House became Greenwich Hospital School, along with a new strip of land from taken the park so that it had its own grounds. Montagu house became the new Ranger's lodging.

---

53   Survey of London Monograph 14, the Queen's House, Greenwich.

Montagu House

In the South West corner of the park close to the Rose Garden are some remnants of a house that used to stand just outside the boundary of the park, so close in fact, that it made use of the park wall as one of its own walls [Map: K2].

It was, by all accounts, an unimpressive house which had been built in the second half of the seventeenth century as a country retreat for Ralph Montagu, First Duke of Montagu and Master of the Horse for Queen Catherine, wife of Charles II. His main residence in Bloomsbury, also called Montagu House, was bought by the government to display its collection of antiquities and is now the site of the British Museum.

The house in Greenwich remained in the hands of the Montagu family for two generations, the second Duke of Montagu marrying Lady Mary Churchill, part of the Marlborough dynasty from which Winston Churchill was descended.

Image 83: The end of Montagu House, looking north west, in 1786 PD

Ignatius Sancho

The most notable resident of Montagu House was the self-educated writer and composer Ignatius Sancho who was the butler to Mary Churchill, Lady Montagu. A plaque on the original wall of the house next to Queen Caroline's Bath celebrates his life [Map: K2].

He was born on a slave ship in 1729 that was taking his parents to New Grenada, where he was baptised and given his Christian name. His mother died soon after their arrival and his distraught father committed suicide. When he was two, his owner brought him to England and gave him to three sisters in Blackheath to look after. They gave him the surname Sancho because they felt he looked like the squire from Don Quixote. Although he was no longer a slave, or treated badly, he was considered to be very inferior by the sisters and denied any education.

Image 84: Ignatius Sancho by Thomas Gainsborough, 1768 PD

During his regular social outings, the Duke of Montagu had met him and been impressed by his charm and natural abilities. He invited him to Montagu House regularly as a guest and offered him an education and gifts of books, much to the annoyance of the three sisters.

When the Duke died in 1749, the twenty year old Ignatius despaired as he had grown to love his time at Montagu House. He pleaded with Lady Montagu to take him into her employment, which she did, giving him the role of butler in her household. He remained butler until her death in 1751, upon which he received a generous annuity of thirty pounds and had also accumulated seventy pounds in savings[54].

---

54 Approximately £7,000 and £16,000 respectively in today's terms.

Unfortunately, these meagre riches seduced him into many acts of folly, and gambling led to him squandering his wealth. However, throughout this, he maintained his love of the arts and became a frequent visitor to the theatre, even auditioning for a role as Othello. In 1758 he married Anne Osborn and in 1761 the first of his seven children was born.

By 1766 he had returned to employment at Montagu House as valet to the husband of Lady Montagu's daughter, originally having been retained by the family chaplain. It was during this time that he began to write letters. One of his first was to Laurence Sterne[55] from whom he sought help in publicising the issue of racism and gain support for the abolition of slavery. In 1767 he self-published a collection of minuets, cotillions and country dances dedicated to the Duke and anonymously attributed to 'an African'. He went on to publish three other volumes of music.

When he reached 44, he was finding the physical work of a valet too difficult as he had become unhealthy with gout. Using his savings, he bought a shop in Mayfair which the Duke helped him to find, and he and his wife began to sell groceries to the well-to-do. Not only could he now enjoy intellectual conversations with his customers, he was also a financially independent man with property. This meant that he was entitled to vote in the general election of 1774, becoming the first black man to exercise that right.

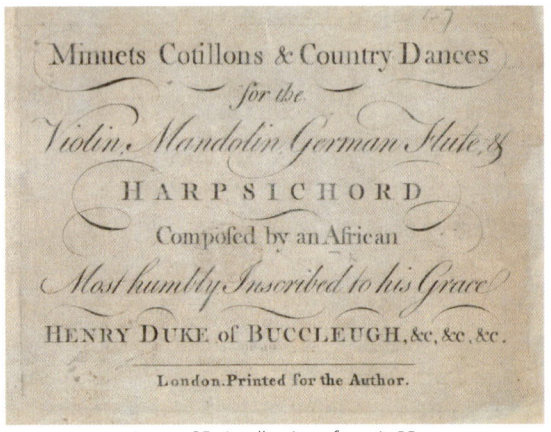

Image 85: A collection of music PD

In 1775 Laurence Sterne died and their correspondence was published. Suddenly he was famous and had a reputation as a learned man of letters. He seized this opportunity to become an outspoken evangelist and role model for the abolition of slavery. By the time he died in 1780, he was so well known that he had his obituary published in the newspapers, another first for a black Englishman.

---

55   The author of Tristram Shandy

Caroline of Brunswick

In 1798 Montagu House became home to Caroline of Brunswick, the wife of the future George IV, who was still the Prince of Wales at the time. Her arranged marriage to George in 1795 was bitter and divided from the outset and George did everything he could to make life difficult for her. Consequently, after the birth of her daughter Charlotte in 1797, she lived separately from him, first at Shrewsbury House in Shooters Hill, then at Montagu House. In 1805 it became clear that the couple would never be reconciled and the king, George III, appointed her Park Ranger.

Image 86: Caroline of Brunswick. PD

Since the Queen's House was in disrepair, Caroline remained in Montagu house. In 1806, she used her status as the Park Ranger to enclose the surrounding five acres of the still private park for her personal use and indulge in her favourite pastime of gardening. This included a sunken grove near the south west entrance called The Dell which later became part of the American garden.

The feud with her husband continued with each of them trying to outdo each other in the outrageous things that they did. When George refused to let her see her daughter, Caroline carried on, but it eventually became too much for her, and she moved to Italy in 1814.

Montagu House was not deemed suitable as a residence for the Park Ranger and it was demolished to enlarge the grounds of the neighbouring Chesterfield House which had been acquired for that purpose, becoming known as the Ranger's House in the process. The only parts of Montagu House remaining are a plunge bath and the wall behind it in which you can see the bricked up spaces where a door and windows were once located.

Queen Caroline's Bath

This bath is a rather unusual remnant of Montagu House and was only fully excavated in 2001. It was rediscovered in 1890, when a dilapidated summer house was removed from the site. The summer house, which stood over the bath, was built of wood, with a slate roof. It had fitted seats around the interior and may have been the much repaired original [Map: K2].

The bath is deep enough to stand up in and a large part is taken up by eight full size steps to allow the bather to get in and out easily. The original white tiles are still affixed to the walls in the lower parts, the upper sections having been stripped out to repair the interior of the old summerhouse. The bath house and adjoining glasshouse were a generous size being around 8m by 5m and would have originally been constructed of glass and a light wooden latticework frame.

Image 87: Queen Caroline's Bath

A lead pipe fifty millimetres in diameter was used to fill the bath and probably connected to the kitchen or laundry, but there was no drain and a small lead lined spherical indent in the corner of the floor was probably a sump to assist with pumping the water out.

Bathing was a Georgian institution and considered extremely healthy. Many spa towns, such as Bath and Buxton, grew prosperous during this period from visitors enjoying their public bathing houses and mineral waters. George IV, Caroline's estranged husband, even built the Royal Pavilion in Brighton. On Shooters Hill, just four kilometres from Montagu House, Epsom Salts were produced from natural springs and the waters were used in spas. No doubt some of that invigorating water made its way here.

The Delicate Investigation

Caroline's arranged marriage to the Prince of Wales was a sham as George had already illegally married a member of the court called Maria Fitzherbert. Instead of wallowing in self-pity, Caroline was strong willed and determined to escape the repression she experienced during her childhood. She threw herself into society and established her own circle of friends and lovers, hosting parties and masquerade balls which were as outrageous and sexually charged as those of her errant husband.

Her 'unladylike' activities were brought into the open through a much publicised scandal called 'The Delicate Investigation'. This centred around her apparent purchase of a child that she then told people was hers, causing constitutional concerns, as the child would be an heir to the throne. The report concluded that the child was not hers, but cited much circumstantial evidence that she was guilty of adultery, leaving her reputation in tatters. The king and George broke off all relations with her, but she remained a popular figure in Britain and counted Jane Austin as one of her many supporters, saying of her:

"*Poor woman, I shall support her as long as I can, because she is a woman and because I hate her husband.*"

The Dell

In 1898 the Dell and American Garden lying along the south west wall of the park were replanted with a large collection of flowering shrubs including buddleia and rhododendrons [Map: K3]. A rockery was also added as a feature near to the Blackheath gate [Map: K4].

Image 88: The Rockery

At the same time the adjacent playing field was turned into a cricket pitch and this now has a small cricket pavilion as well [Map: K3].

Image 89: A relaxing game of cricket

Ranger's House

Image 90: Ranger's House

The Ranger's House was built between 1722-23 for Captain Francis Hosier in a simple Palladian style and was one of the first houses to be sited on Blackheath bounding the park. The location of the house would have given him excellent views over all the nautical activities in Greenwich and on the Thames [Map: J2].

Hosier was born in Deptford and joined the navy in 1685, working his way up to the rank of vice admiral. He made his fortune in 1710 when he was captain of The Salisbury and captured a much larger French ship called Le Heureux off the southern coast of Ireland.

He died in 1727 of fever caught while blockading the Spanish in the West Indies at Porto Bello leaving behind his wife and daughter. Sadly the ownership of the house was contested and it took until 1740 for it to pass to his mother's family at which point it was immediately leased to the Earl of Chesterfield and became known as Chesterfield House.

On the Earl's death, his son, Lord Chesterfield, took over the lease and had the building extensively remodelled, turning it into his favourite villa. It was at this time that the avenue of trees outside the park called Chesterfield Walk that runs parallel to the park wall was created.

Chesterfield House was purchased by the Crown in 1815 and refurbished to become the new Ranger's House and suitable for Princess Sophia Matilda, the aunt of Queen Victoria, who took residence. She was a great philanthropist and very popular with the people of Greenwich who saw her as a kind and generous benefactor to the town's poor. When she died in 1844 her elaborate funeral procession from the Ranger's House into Greenwich drew large crowds.

In 1902 the last Ranger left the house, the role of Park Ranger having been abolished by parliament. Now English Heritage own the house and have installed the collection of Julius Wernher who made his fortune from South African diamonds, being one of the founders of the famous De Beers company. Wernher never lived in Ranger's House, but those that did used it to house their personal collections. When visiting today his quirky collection makes the house appear complete, almost as if Julius Wernher was the last, but posthumous, Greenwich Park Ranger.

Macartney House

Just along from the Ranger's House is Macartney House which is still a private residence, but converted into a number of flats [Map: J2]. It was built in 1694 and in 1752 the parents of General James Wolfe moved here with their son. He was 25 years old at the time, but already a highly regarded lieutenant-colonel in the British Army. Although he had been born in Westerham in Kent, he had lived most of his life in Greenwich and regarded it as his home.

He died in 1759 while leading from the front during his decisive victory over the French at Quebec and his statue can be found outside the Royal Observatory.

After the battle his body was brought back to Greenwich and laid in state at Macartney House before finally being interred in the crypt of St. Alfege's Church.

The White House

Another historic and listed private house stands besides the path leading to the Croom's Hill gate entrance to the park [Map: H2]. This building, which lives up to its name with its white painted walls, was once the home of the seventh Astronomer Royal, Sir George Biddell Airy.

It was required that he lived in the observatory while he held the position, but on his retirement he moved his family here, as close as he could be to the place that had been the centre of his life for so long. His wife, her sisters, and his daughter Christabel, were all talented artists who made many studies of life at the observatory during their time living there. Christabel, who never married, remained in the White House until her death in 1917.

Image 91: Painting of the observatory by Christabel Airy who lived at the White House and spent a lot of time at the observatory. This picture shows the original roof of the Great Equatorial Observatory PD

The Queen's House

Image 92: The Queen's House on a frosty morning.

The Queen's House is so integral to the history of Greenwich Park that it warrants a detailed description.

When built, the Queen's House was unlike anything seen in England before. Not only was it the first Palladian style villa in the country, with its mathematically balanced proportions, but it was also faced with white rusticated stone at a time when all the surrounding buildings were red brick, and was frequently referred to as the White House.

Until the development of the Naval Hospital, it stood on its own, dominating the park, with the main Greenwich to Woolwich road running underneath it, exactly where the colonnades are now. The southern half of the house jutted out into the park and the northern half into the formal gardens of the Palace of Placentia. As such, it provided a luxurious bridge between the two areas.

The building has had many uses over the years: palace; school; residence;

museum and offices for the 2012 Olympic Games, so much of the interior of the building has been reconstructed, but all the restoration has been faithful to the original designs of Inigo Jones.

The Queen's House is currently an art gallery containing just a small part of the National Maritime Museum collection which includes several historical views of Greenwich Park and the old palaces and buildings. You will also find portraits of many of the historical figures associated with Greenwich, including the instantly recognisable Armada portrait of Elizabeth I and Holbein's representation of her father, the ageing Henry VIII.

The Loggia

The Loggia, or long veranda, that overlooks the park is best viewed from within the park. Facing south, it would have been a delightful place on a warm summer's day to admire the view over the park and, had they ever been laid-out, the formal gardens of the parterre.

The Loggia was built longer than those typical of Palladio as Inigo Jones considered it to be one of the finest features of a house and invested a lot of time in making it a show-piece of the building.

The Great Hall

It is not just the outside where the building adheres to the strict rules of proportion and symmetry that Palladian architecture dictates. The Great Hall with its high ceiling, original marble floor and central gallery, is a perfect cube with every side 40 feet (12.2m).

The black and white marble floor is original and was laid in 1637 by Nicholas Stone and Gabriel Stacey following the design of Inigo Jones.

The gallery, which runs all around the hall suspended on oak cantilever brackets typical of the period, is also original, but has had to be extensively repaired and reinforced. The gilded paintwork is also largely original, having been revealed after the removal of many layers of paint in 1925. The ceiling mouldings would have been similarly painted.

Image 93: The Great Hall in the Queen's House. The marble floor and balustrades are original.

The ceiling, in white and gold leaf, is a new feature from the latest refurbishment and was created by Richard Wright using traditional methods. White and gold were the colours of Henrietta Maria and the Great Hall was finished in these colours when it was occupied by her.

The ceiling originally displayed nine specially commissioned paintings by Orazio Gentileschi and his daughter Artemesia, but these were removed in 1708 before the building was leased to the Naval Hospital and given to Sarah Churchill as a present. They can still be seen on the ceiling in Marlborough House in London when it is open to the public.

Tulip Staircase

Just outside the Great Hall is the Tulip Staircase, the first example of a cantilevered spiral staircase in England. It has no central support making it airy and light and is also an original feature. It takes its name from its decorative blue iron work where each panel is filled with a graceful curving tulip design. You can take this staircase up to the

Image 94: The Tulip Staircase in the Queen's House

first floor and then visit the gallery and main exhibition rooms, but you will notice that the stairs also continue up to the roof which is flat and leaded and originally accessible.

From the gallery you can get a really good impression of the cubic shape of the Great Hall and also access the King's and Queen's Presence Chambers.

The King's Presence Chamber has blue walls, the same colour as the Tulip Stairs, and the mouldings on the walls and ceiling are highlighted in gold leaf creating a very royal feel. The room has had many modifications and only the ceiling decorations are original.

The Queen's Presence Chamber has rich red walls on which hangs the Armada Portrait dominating the room, but don't forget to look up at the ceiling. It was painted in what is referred to as the Italian Grotesque style and is called Aurora Dispersing the Shades of Night. It was installed about 50 years after the house was completed by the relatively obscure Edward Pierce Senior.

The Armada Portrait

This painting of Elizabeth I is familiar to most people, but the story behind it is less well known.

The Armada Portrait marks the astonishing defeat of the Spanish Armada by the English navy under the leadership of Sir Francis Drake. Many copies were painted to be sent around her realm and send a clear message about the power of Elizabeth I after this great victory.

Image 95: Armada Portrait of Elizabeth I

This is one of three remaining versions, and by an unknown artist. Behind the queen on the left is the English fleet in neat formation, and on the right, the Spanish fleet floundering in a storm. This was a key message as it showed how God was on Elizabeth and England's side.

Spain and England had been enemies ever since Henry VIII divorced Catherine of Aragon. When the pope declared Elizabeth I an enemy of the Church, the devout Spanish King, Phillip II, invoked God's will and assembled an army of allies and a fleet of more than 120 ships to invade England. The Armada, which carried 8,000 sailors and 18,000 soldiers, set sail under the leadership of the Duke of Medina Sidonia in May 1588. It would sail through the English Channel to pick up 30,000 more troops from Holland, creating an overwhelming invasion force.

The English spotted the fleet and harried them as they progressed up the channel. Although the Spanish were heavily armed, the English fleet had two advantages: it was more agile and it could reload and fire its cannons quickly. Weaving in and out of the Spanish ships, the English unleashed repeated broadsides on their targets while receiving little returning fire themselves. With heavy casualties and much structural damage the Armada was forced to anchor off Calais to regroup.

At midnight, with favourable winds, the English sent eight fire ships[56] towards the anchored Spanish Fleet. Six made it into the heart of the Armada and most of the Spanish ships cut anchor fearing they would explode. The strong westerly winds carried them into the North Sea away from their destination and they were forced to abandon the invasion and head home.

Comfortable that the threat was over, Queen Elizabeth spoke to troops at the fort of Tilbury saying the famous words: "I know I have the body of a weak, feeble woman; but I have the heart and stomach of a king, and of a king of England too".

The only way home for the Armada was around Scotland and Ireland. Without anchors or good maps, storms sunk half the fleet and killed three quarters of the men, turning a failure into a complete disaster.

---

56 An empty ship set ablaze to drift into an enemy's fleet. Sometimes barrels of gunpowder were stashed below deck which would cause delayed explosions.

A Park for the People

Since its enclosure in 1437 the park had been owned by the Crown and was off limits to the general population except by invitation. This remained the case until the start of the eighteenth century when the development of the Naval Hospital meant that there was no longer a royal palace in Greenwich. Although the park and Queen's House continued to be owned by the Crown, it was no longer used by the royal family, and the governors of the Naval Hospital began to have more influence over the park than even the Ranger.

Local residents were able to request access and required a small coin sized copper token to show to the gatekeepers[57].

The bigger houses neighbouring the park had keys to their nearest gate, and some Naval College houses had their own gate like those at the foot of Maze Hill. Others could also gain entry despite these measures because access was not very effectively policed, so, to all intents and purposes, anyone could get into the park if they so wished.

There were several days each year when the entire park was thrown open to the public, and these included the six days of the two annual Greenwich Fairs which were such a significant event in London that they were extensively written about in contemporary literature.

When George IV became king in 1820 he declared the park to be a public park. Although access was only permitted during daylight hours as today, anyone could now officially enjoy a walk and take in the views.

---

57 From A.D. Webster

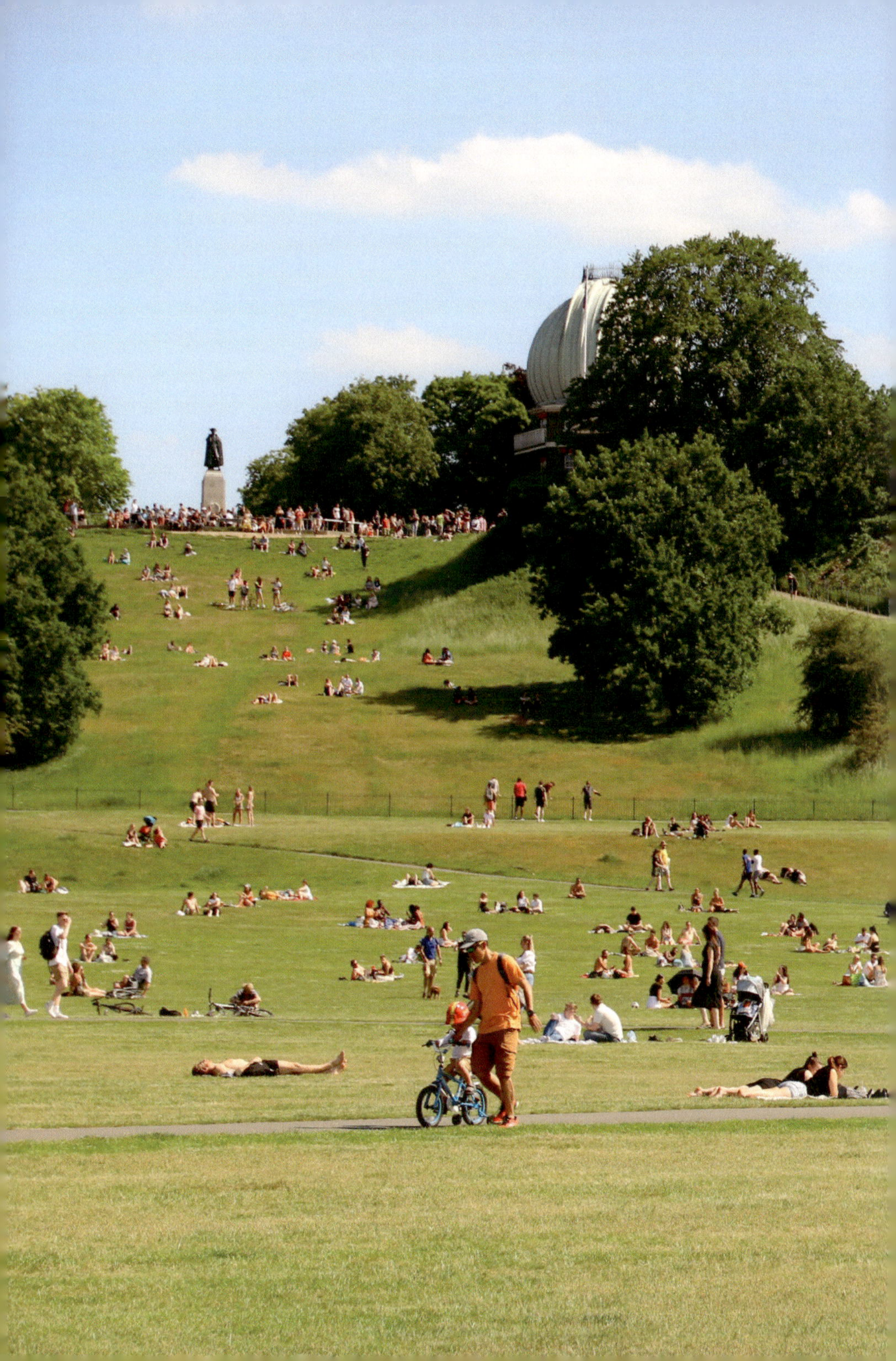

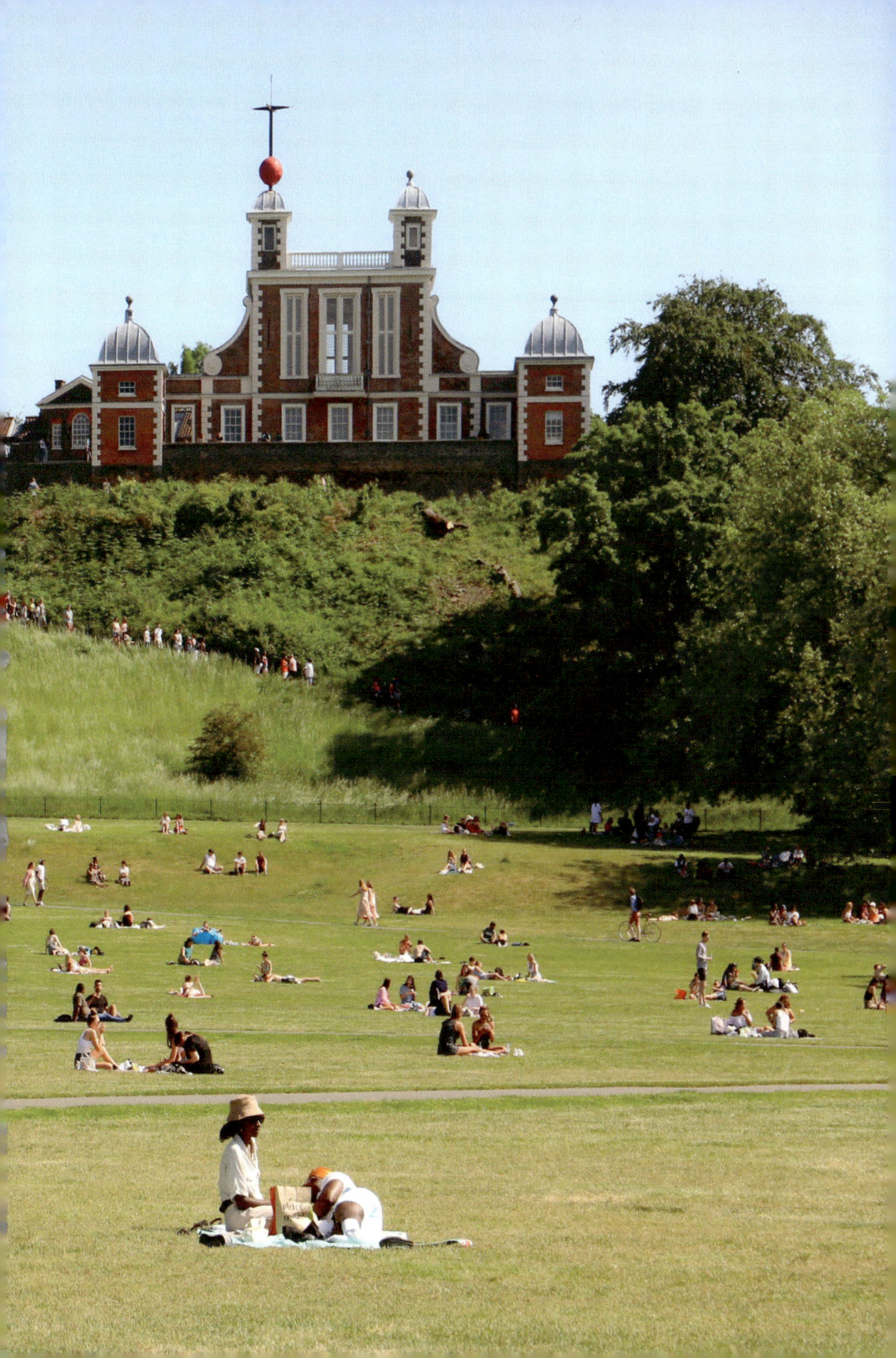

Greenwich Fair

Today fun fairs still take place regularly on Blackheath which had for many years been the site of a large agricultural fair with a charter from the king. This modern event is, however, a pale imitation of the original Greenwich Fair which became a great London institution.

Origin and Growth

Fairs became a very common form of entertainment in medieval England, often associated with religious days or agricultural trading. As with Blackheath, permission to hold them was usually granted by a royal charter, but Greenwich Fair, which originally took place in May, before settling on Easter and Whitsun, appears to have never been chartered and was a permissive event[58]. It is unlikely that it existed before 1700 as neither Samuel Pepys nor John Evelyn mention it in their diaries despite their strong associations with Greenwich and several recorded visits to other fairs, such as the Bartholomew Fair.

Although Henry VIII and Elizabeth I held many spectacular events during their time in Greenwich, the first mention of a truly public fair is by the French novelist Voltaire who visited London in May 1726 and disembarked in Greenwich while it was in progress.

I landed near Greenwich, on the banks of the Thames... Close to the river, on a large greensward which extends for about four miles, I saw an immense number of comely young people cajoling on horseback... I was fortunate enough to meet in the crowd some merchants to whom I had letters of introduction... They took the trouble to put me in a place where I could easily see all the incidents in the races, with the river close by, and a view of London in the distance. A [visitor who sat next to me] from Denmark believed that the entire nation was always gay, that all the women were sprightly and beautiful, and that the sky of England was always pure and serene[59].

By the time of Voltaire's visit the park had been out of favour with the Royal Family for some time and had become neglected. In 1743 Lady Catherine Pelham

---

58 Many fairs were permitted to take place without a charter because they were established events.
59 Much shortened from Voltaire's visit to England, 1726-1729.

was appointed Park Ranger and, after taking residence in the Queen's House, she began to restore the park which, although still private property, was becoming much more open to the people of Greenwich. On fair days and other public holidays it was formally open to the general public with men on the main gates supervising access.

The fair continued to grow in popularity largely because it was early in the year making it the first big event of each new season after the long, dark and cold winter. It began to attract all sorts of travelling curiosities and entertainments. In 1748 a newspaper carried an advertisement for a menagerie containing a camel, hyena, panther and several other beasts that would be displayed at the Rose and Crown pub near to the gates of Greenwich Park.[60] This drinking establishment was later to extend into a music hall and, after several rebuilds, become Greenwich Theatre.

Image 96: Sign from the Rose and Crown Pub by Greenwich Theatre

As the fair grew in popularity it expanded to take over the centre of Greenwich and the Naval Hospital made available the extensive waste ground that bounded the park at its north west corner where Nevada Street and King William Walk are today. The commissioners of the Royal Hospital happily supported and encouraged the fair since they shared the receipts from the rental of stands with the town constable.

Eventually, even this space was not enough, and the fair began to spread west, running along Creek Road as far as Deptford Bridge.

---

60 The Old Showmen and the Old London Fairs, by Thomas Frost.

Victorians

During the Victorian era it was estimated that 200,000 people were attending the fair. Its dates had been changed to coincide with the major public holidays of Easter and Whitsun, taking place on the Monday, Tuesday and Wednesday of each week. By 1818 the fair had become especially popular amongst the working classes and featured a number of travelling theatres, dance halls and other attractions. By 1825, it had become so rowdy, that magistrates attempted to suppress it, and banned it from taking place in the park. Although the theatres were not present that year, the dance halls and drinking booths were erected outside the park extending along the road to Deptford and the fair carried on regardless[61], returning to normal the following year.

Part of the whole fair-going experience was to take a paddle steamer[62] from the Port of London to Greenwich Pier from where you then had to make your way up to the park. The first obstacle was getting past the overflowing Ship Tavern[63] and after that the rows of stalls and waggons lining the streets and intent on selling you food and trinkets.

The popularity of the event across London was highlighted on Good Friday when the streets were full of boys selling hot cross buns.

The sellers of the Good Friday buns are principally boys, and they are of mixed classes, costers' boys, boys habitually street-sellers, and boys street-sellers for that occasion only. One great inducement to embark in the trade is the hope of raising a little money for the Greenwich Fair of the following Monday[64].

Who better to give us a real sense of what those boys were hoping to enjoy than Charles Dickens who, in 1836, published "Sketches by Boz" which included some well written description of Greenwich Fair illustrated by his friend George Cruikshank.

---

61 The Old Showmen and the Old London Fairs, by Thomas Frost
62 Paddle steamers were a very popular day out in Victorian London, but they were notoriously overcrowded and unsafe. In 1878 the Princess Alice sank after a collision off Woolwich and 650 people were drowned in the heavily polluted Thames.
63 Originally The Torbay Tavern, it became part of the Ship Hotel which stood roughly where the Cutty Sark ship is located today and was a large Inn with balconies.
64 Henry Mayhew 1851

Five minutes' walking brings you to the fair; a scene calculated to awaken very different feelings. The entrance is occupied on either side by the vendors of gingerbread and toys: the stalls are gaily lighted up, the most attractive goods profusely disposed, and unbonneted young ladies, in their zeal for the interest of their employers, seize you by the coat, and use all the blandishments of 'Do, dear'—'There's a love'—'Don't be cross, now,' etc., to induce you to purchase half a pound of the real spice nuts.

The chief place of resort in the daytime, after the public-houses, is the park, in which the principal amusement is to drag young ladies up the steep hill which leads to the observatory, and then drag them down again, at the very top of their speed, greatly to the derangement of their curls and bonnet-caps, and much to the edification of lookers-on from below. 'Kiss in the Ring,' and 'Threading my Grandmother's Needle,' too, are sports which receive their full share of patronage. Lovesick swains, under the influence of gin-and-water, and the tender passion, become violently affectionate: and the fair objects of their regard enhance the value of stolen kisses, by a vast deal of struggling, and holding down of heads.

The grandest and most numerously-frequented booth in the whole fair, however, is 'The Crown and Anchor', a temporary ball-room, we forget how many hundred feet long, the price of admission to which is one shilling. Immediately on your right hand as you enter, after paying your money, is a refreshment place, at which cold beef, roast and boiled, French rolls, stout, wine, tongue, ham, even fowls, if we recollect right, are displayed in tempting array. There is a raised orchestra, and the place is boarded all the way down, in patches, just wide enough for a country dance. There is no master of the ceremonies in this artificial Eden, all is primitive, unreserved, and unstudied. The dust is blinding, the heat insupportable, the company somewhat noisy, and in the highest spirits possible: the ladies, in the height of their innocent animation, dancing in the gentlemen's hats, and the gentlemen promenading 'the gay and festive scene' in the ladies' bonnets.

Imagine yourself in an extremely dense crowd, which swings you to and fro, and in and out, and every way but the right one; add to this the screams of women, the shouts of boys, the clanging of gongs, the firing of pistols, the ringing of bells, the bellowings of speaking-trumpets, the squeaking of penny dittos, the noise of a dozen bands, with three drums in each, all playing different tunes at the same time, the hallooing of showmen, and an occasional roar from the wild-beast shows; and you are in the very centre and heart of the fair.

Menageries

An extremely popular show during the Victorian era was the menagerie, or animal show. The highlight was invariably a lion tamer or 'Lion King'. Greenwich Fair had many competing events including the two largest travelling shows, Wombwell's and Hilton's[65].

Competition was great and new spectacles were always needed to attract the crowds. In 1840 George Hilton introduced his daughter as a lion tamer, and, as the first 'Lion Queen', Polly Hilton quickly became the must-see show at all fairs. Following suit George Wombwell made his niece, Ellen Bright, a Lion Queen, but after she was savaged and killed by a tiger[66] in 1850, Lion Queens were banned.

In 1857 a black sailor visiting Greenwich Fair approached William Manders, who had taken over Hilton's Menagerie, about becoming a lion tamer. Being

---

65 The Old Showmen and the Old London Fairs, by Thomas Frost
66 Ellen Bright died from tiger inflicted wounds in Chatham after a private show to naval officers, not Greenwich as stated by Thomas Frost.

unsatisfied with the current incumbent he gave him a trial. Martini Maccomo, as he became known, was exceptionally daring and popular, touring the country long after Greenwich Fair had been closed.

The End of Greenwich Fair

The Victorian era is renowned for its hypocritical prudishness and disdainful attitude to the poor. By 1857 Greenwich Fair, along with many others, had been banned by act of parliament. A clue to the thinking of the time was given by William Sanger in 1897.

Greenwich Fair, a three days' scene of rollicking and junketing, was held at Easter and Whitsuntide, in the outskirts of London, but is now abolished. It had its uses a century or two ago, but recently had been attended by all the idlers of London, of both sexes, and was justly dreaded by the friends of youth. It is proverbial that more young women were debauched at Greenwich Fair (allowing for its duration) than at any other place in England.

Several ditties were written in memory of the fair, of which Poor Old Greenwich Fair captures the mood of those deprived of their fun.

Image 97: Attributed to: W. Dover, 18, Gt. St Andrew Street, Seven Dials. PD

Poor Old Greenwich Fair

When at Easter and at Whitsuntide we used to go so gay,
By wind and steam so merrily to pass dull care away.
Now at Easter and at Whitsuntide, no more we shall repair,
Oh cruel was the rogues who done away with Greenwich fair,

We used to go to Greenwich fair and there have such a lark,
to see the pretty maidens rolling down through Greenwich park.
Then into the swings they hasten and go flying in the air,
There was never such a pretty place as poor old Greenwich fair.

There was roasted pigs and nanny-goats in Greenwich fair was sold,
There was hats and ladies' bustles trim'd with California Gold,
There was lovely cocks & bretches, saveloys & hot pea soup,
Three sticks a penny, in the hole and pricking in the loop*[1].

What lots of fun and humour used to be at Greenwich fair,
There was Billy Punch and Judy too in all their glory there.
There was firing at the target and lollipops to sell,
And private rooms for ladies to play at bagatelle*[2].

I never shall forget the time, and I'm sure will never you,
When old Brown upon his salt box used to play the rat*[3] too.
Last Friday night the Baker's wife did solemnly declare,
She saw the ghost of Billy Richardson* dancing round the fair.

She saw the ghost of Algiers*[4] too, which made old doughy jump,
He had eleven gas lamps hanging to his rump.
She saw old Woombell's*[4] elephant dancing in the dark,
And then upon the fairground met the ghost of Billy Clark*[4].

Nine pretty maids in Greenwich Park one Easter I did see,
Who wished to look and see a cock*[5] climb up a chestnut tree.
But what a lark, the bough it broke, and they could not hold fast,
When down they came upon their bums, a-rolling on the grass.

Oh cruel was the naughty rogues, how could they ever dare,
To sign a long petition to kill old Greenwich fair.
May they never see a comfort, may they never taste a nut,
May they die upon the river with a scratcher*[6] in their gut.

Old Greenwich was delightful when the shop boys were let loose,
The Barber sold his lather box the tailor sold his goose,
The cobbler sold his lapstone to banish grief and care,
And Sally pawned her linen smock to go to Greenwich fair.

Then weep you lads and lasses, lie down and shed a tear,
And cry 'oh dear', we never more shall see old Greenwich fair.

* 1: Fairground games. 2: Similar to billiards and popular with women. 3: Skipping work or school. 4: Richardson's theatre, Clarke's circus, Wombwell's menagerie and Algar's Crown and Anchor brightly lit dance hall were all popular sources of entertainment. 5: A cock-sure, or brash, youth. 6: A small narrow bladed knife designed for stabbing.

Attracting Visitors

The Bandstand

Image 98: The Bandstand, still entertaining park visitors after 130 years.

As the industrial revolution brought more and more people into the cramped cities and their unhealthy, overcrowded slums, Victorian town planners recognised the importance of open spaces like parks to maintain good health and public order and wanted to encourage the population to use them. The idea of brass bands playing free concerts in purpose-built bandstands proved extremely popular and soon became an essential feature of any respectable Victorian park [Map: H5].

The Greenwich Park bandstand is made of cast iron and follows a standard format that was used across the whole of Britain. It was assembled on site in 1891 having been cast in sections at the famous Coalbrookdale works in Shropshire, where Abraham Darby had first set up his coke fired blast furnace in 1709, the start of the modern iron industry.

With their thirst for music satisfied, the audience could visit a granite water fountain on the intersection of Blackheath Avenue and Great Cross Avenue which was also installed in 1891 and supplied by Alex McDonald of Aberdeen. This can be found in the same position today in the middle of the car park, but currently does not work.

In the summer the bandstand still occasionally hosts brass bands, as well as more unusual ensembles, most often on a Sunday. Being a landmark and raised space, it is also used as a focal point for many of the events that take place in the park.

Image 99 The granite fountain

Pavilion Tea House

The Pavilion Tea House was opened in 1907 and was designed by Sir Henry Tanner who was the Principal Surveyor of the London Office of Works. It is a charming octagonal building with a decorative dovecote that has a wind vane depicting a man with a telescope. It is one of four weather vanes in the vicinity here so there is no excuse for not knowing the direction of the wind [Map: H4].

When it was originally built the only enclosed part was the centre of the building which housed the kitchen, toilets and stairs to the upper floor. Today's glazed exterior is a later addition, and prior to that, the seating was open to the air and sheltered by the upper story. This was also used for seating and had a cast iron balustrade running around it for safety. Although this upper floor is not open today, the tea room still has extensive gardens for alfresco eating, and is consequently very popular in the summer months.

Image 100: The Pavilion Tea Room as originally designed. PD

Image 101: The Pavilion Cafe in Corona Virus mode in 2021 serving take away drinks only.

Boating Lake

Image 102: A pedalo on the boating lake.

The boating lake is found just inside the Park Row entrance. If you are visiting in the summer you can hire a pedalo, but during the winter, it is drained for maintenance reasons [Map: D5].

It was established along with one in Regent's Park in 1930 and was officially opened by Sir George Lansbury on 20th June. Sir George was a socialist reformer and an East End Member of Parliament for the Labour Party. When Labour formed a minority government in 1929 he was appointed as First Commissioner of Works and had responsibility for the Royal Parks. With the country entering the great economic depression, he commissioned many improvements to the parks, including the boating lake in Greenwich. He was a champion for women's rights and changed the law so that it was no longer illegal for women to bathe in the parks and is celebrated for building the Lido on the Serpentine in Hyde Park with affordable changing facilities.

In 2012 the boating lake featured in the Olympics as a water jump for the equestrian cross country event. The horses entered from the south west corner, turned, jumped and exited in the south east corner.

Sundial

On the north side of the boating lake is a sundial which was designed by Chris Daniel and installed in 1999 to mark the new millennium. It is positioned on the meridian line and has a Double Horizontal Dial showing both the time and the direction of the sun [Map: D5].

The dial plate looks like a clock and is labelled with Roman numerals from which you can read the time cast by the large brass triangle known as the gnomon.

The time is indicated by the shadow made by the sloping outside edge of the gnomon, and the direction of the sun by the shadow from the vertical edge. The shadow does not always reach the dial so you have to extend the line visually.

Sundials should be accurate to within five minutes depending on the time of year. This one is quite simple and so is most accurate in the summer. You must remember to add on one hour because, quite appropriately for its location on the meridian, it tells the time in GMT.

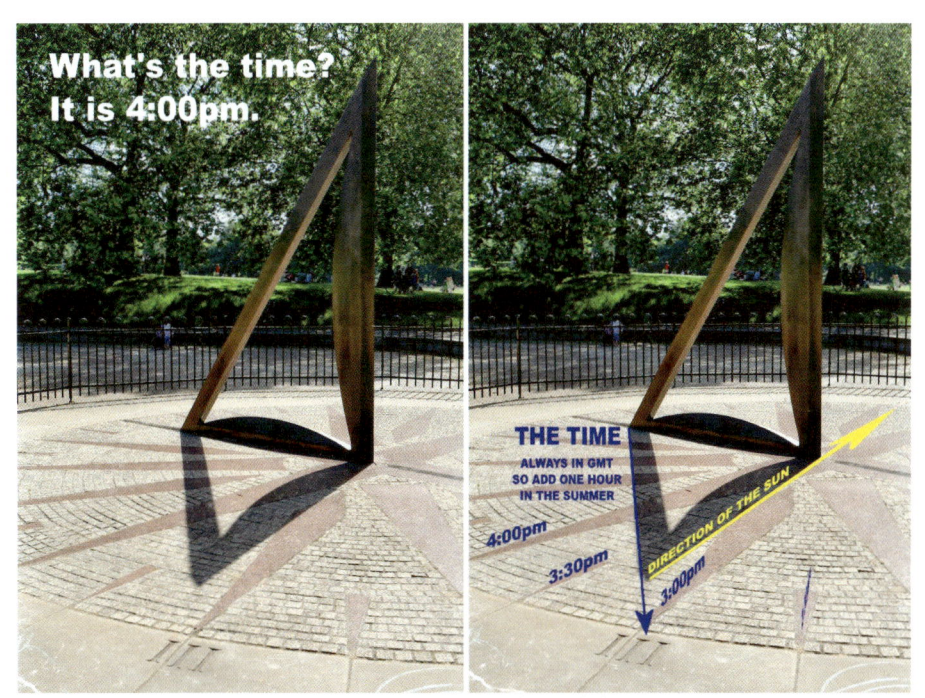

Image 103: How to use the sundial.

Playground

Just beyond the boating lake is the playground which is extremely well equipped and very popular with young families [Map: E6]. It is one of the most visited places in the park along with the observatory terrace.

It was once a very neglected area but at the start of the twentieth century it became dedicated to children's play in the form of a large sand pit. These were quite common in urban parks and popular with children, often being referred to as 'the seaside'. Many also had a paddling pool, but this was not the case in Greenwich Park.

Image 104: 'Seaside in Greenwich Park' c.1907. At that time the north east corner of the park was not well used. PD

Just south of the playground there was a small pond which had become stagnant and unpleasant. This was filled-in in 1857.

Image 105: The modern playground, empty because it was closed due to high winds.

Under the Park

Before the advent of modern utility services, places that required a significant and regular supply of fresh water had to provide their own. The easiest method was to obtain it from a nearby stream, spring or well. In Greenwich, the geology meant that these options were not available and instead rain water falling on the high ground had to be captured and stored in a private reservoir.

The manor house of Old Court, built by the Abbey of Ghent in the thirteenth century, had been large enough to have its own water supplied via a conduit system which was subsequently known as the Arundell Conduit. This ran from the high ground east of the park to the river and later supplied water to the Tudor stables that were adjacent to Old Court[67]. There is no trace of it today.

When Humphrey, Duke of Gloucester built Bella Court in 1434 he was given permission by King Henry VI to build a conduit from the existing public well in Greenwich to his new home. It is known that this well was fed by conduits that conveyed water from Blackheath and the high ground of the park into Greenwich. This public well, or stockwell[68], was situated on the edge of Greenwich Park almost directly opposite the present day 14 Croom's Hill and dates back to the thirteenth century.

Today three conduits are known to still run through the park, but a survey in 1695 that was investigating the best way to provide water for the new Naval Hospital, reported that there were eight conduits in the area. Following this survey, those conduits that could be used were rebuilt to an impressive standard, being paved, lined with brick and made tall enough for a man to walk upright in to allow for easy maintenance.

In the nineteenth century further improvements meant that some of the conduit routes were replaced by iron piping, but the park remains full of remnants of the old conduit system that lies under the surface. It is these artefacts that are often the least well understood aspects of the park.

---

67 St. Peter's Abbey, Ghent by Julian Watson, Greenwich Historical Society
68 This well gives Stockwell Street its name

Conduits and other water supply features in Greenwich Park
Key
Artefact no longer existing.
Artefact still present with known location, but not necessarily visible.
Possible route of a conduit.
Known of very likely route of a conduit
PLACENTIA
CONVENT
CHURCH
Royal Naval College
Possible path for Duke Humphrey of Gloucester's aqueduct
Cutty Sark
Market
Nelson Rd
Romney Rd
St. Alfege's Church
King William Walk
Stockwell St
Maritime Museum
Queen's House
Park Row
PARK ROW
ST. MARY'S
GATE
Vicarage Conduit
Park Vista
The Queen's Orchard
CREED PLACE
Herbaceous Border
Boating Lake
Playground
Stockwell
Crooms Hill
CIRCUS
Herb Garden
JUBILEE AVENUE
THE PARTERRE
Manholes
Conduit Head
One Tree Hill
Maze Hill
MAZE HILL HOUSE
KING GEORGE STREET
Site of old Conduit Head
Conduit House
Standard House
Vent
Standard Reservoir
LOVERS WALK
CROSS AVENUE
GIANT STEPS
Royal Observatory
Reservoir
Site of old Conduit Head
Rustic Fountain
MAZE HILL
Westcombe
Manholes
Queen Elizabeth's Oak
Queen Elizabeth's Bower
Pump Mounting
Keeper's Cottage
Site of Snow well
Manholes
Tumuli
CROOMS HILL
Pavilion Tea House
GREAT CROSS AVENUE
BLACKHEATH AVENUE
Western Admiralty Reservoir
Bandstand
Site of old Conduits
The existing Hyde Vale Conduit Head is about 100m further along Hyde Vale.
Tennis Courts
Ranger's House
Cherry Tree Walk
Flower Garden
BOWER AVENUE
General Wolfe Rd
VANBRUGH PARK
Cricket Pitch
Lake
Chesterfield Walk
The Dell
The Wilderness Deer Enclosure
Charlton Way
CHESTERFIELD
BLACKHEATH

Standard House

Image 106: Standard House conduit

Standard House can be found in the west of the park hidden between the trees of an old avenue called Conduit Avenue. It is the largest and most conspicuous of a number of eighteenth century buildings and artefacts that allowed access to the water in the conduits, and in some cases, to the conduit itself [Map: F2].

It was designed and built by Nicholas Hawksmoor who was overseeing the development of the hospital as the Clerk of Works from 1698 to 1735.

Sometimes called Reservoir Conduit, its purpose was to manage the large underground reservoir that is built in the hillside about 20m behind it, as well as the conduit systems that fed it.

Image 107: Sign on Standard House

Conduit buildings such as these used to be extremely common throughout the country, but only 33 still exist in England and so the three in Greenwich are of great historical significance.

The underground reservoir consists of 8 tanked cells with arched ceilings 2.4 metres high and each being 6 metres long and 2.4 metres wide. The cells are connected together and overall the reservoir has a maximum capacity of more than 250,000 litres. From here the water would have been taken by lead pipes to the hospital.

Image 108: An 'x-ray' view of the reservoir south of Standard House under the rising escarpment Picture is from the east in line with the front of Standard House.

It was filled by one of the largest and best documented conduits (Conduit 51) that runs south-west from the rear of the building before turning south up behind Crooms Hill towards Hyde Vale where another much smaller building called Hyde Vale Conduit Head is located. The immediate route of this conduit is given away by a small square brick venting stack at the back of Standard House on the west side.

On the back wall of Standard House, on either side, is some rather old graffiti which dates back to the eighteenth century and has been carefully carved into the brickwork.

Image 109: Whoever M Penfold was, his graffiti has survived for 250 years! Above can be seen 'James A'.

Slightly further up between the trees there is a concrete block and manhole cover that once provided maintenance access to the reservoir.

The reservoir was made redundant in 1845 when the much larger Western Admiralty Reservoir was opened at the top of the park providing water for both the Naval Hospital and the Naval Shipyard at Deptford. Iron pipes were installed to send the water directly to the hospital.

Although it has not served its original purpose for many years it did find a use during the Second World War as an air raid shelter. Trenches were dug and covered so that entrances could be made in the most easterly and westerly

Image 110: Side of Standard House showing the four wall ties.

chambers and brick passageways covered with concrete slabs were added to provide access to the public. It had lighting installed and twelve toilet cubicles.

With an advertised capacity of 300 people, there would have been no room for bunks, just simple wooden benches, making for an extremely cramped and unpleasant experience until the all clear was sounded. Concerns were eventually raised in parliament that the conditions in many public shelters were so damp, crowded and unhealthy that it might result in more deaths than had the people stayed at home and taken their chances with the bombs.

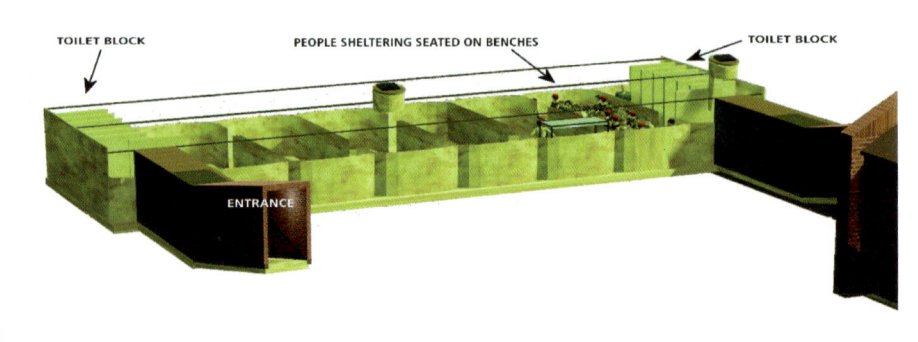

Image 111: Standard House Reservoir in use as an air raid shelter.

There were three additional purpose-built air raid shelters in Greenwich Park in line with government policy of building shelters in parks and other public open spaces. Each had capacity for 300 people and there were entrances at the Vanbrugh Park, Creed Place and St Mary's gates.

Hyde Vale Conduit Head

The conduit system captured water on the high ground through a set of branches from a main conduit. These branches had gaps in their walls so that water in the ground could seep in and begin flowing down to its intended destination under the influence of gravity.

The Hyde Vale conduit (Conduit 51) is exceptionally large and wide and its size has falsely given rise to speculation that it was used as a secret tunnel.

It has several features to improve its performance and accessibility. For example, cavities in the floor were introduced at key points to capture silt that would otherwise eventually block the conduit. These had access points to allow the silt to be removed.

Image 112: Typical conduit showing brick construction and walking height . PD [AD Webster]

The water flowing through this conduit was made accessible near the top of Hyde Vale, just outside the park, through the use of a conduit head. This stands outside the modern building called Conduit House and is a small brick-built semi-cylindrical building about 2.5m high and 1.5m wide. At its base, under a grill, water flowing through the conduit could be extracted.

Despite some later repair work and restoration, the Hyde Vale conduit head remains true to its original design and materials and was constructed about 1710, also by Nicholas Hawksmoor.

Image 113: Hyde Vale Conduit Head.

Queen Elizabeth's Oak Water Pump

Just to the east of Queen Elizabeth's Oak are some large stone slabs set in the ground with a circular metal fitting [Map: G5]. This is all that remains of a large cast iron water pump that the residents of the Keeper's Cottage would have used to extract water from the conduit that runs beneath the slabs.

Image 115: Remains of Water Pump.

Image 114: Queen Elizabeth's Oak in 1900. Note the old water fountain on the right, a remnant of the Keeper's Cottage the fixing plate of which can still be seen today. PD

Underground Reservoir

Halfway between Queen Elizabeth's Oak and Lover's Walk is a tree covered mound that merges into the hillside. It has a manhole cover on the top which provides a clue that something lies beneath. This is top of a reservoir made up of four barrel-vaulted cells dating back to the upgrading of the conduit system, but which was probably substantially altered in the nineteenth century [Map: G5].

The conduit from Queen Elizabeth's Oak feeds this reservoir and it may have been connected to other feeder conduits as well. It is likely that it supplied water to the vicarage conduit house either with a smaller conduit or piping.

The Rustic Fountain

Just off Lover's Walk lies the unusual drinking fountain called the Rustic Fountain cut from two large stones which are probably Kentish Ragstone. Water flowed out of a lead pipe at the back into a bowl shaped hollow. Two metal cups were chained to the fountain to help with drinking and a bolt is present on the left-hand side probably for this purpose. The water was deemed unsafe to drink in the twentieth century and the pipes were sealed [Map: G6]. There are plans to reinstate the water using fresh water from the modern mains supply.

Image 116: Rustic Fountain.

It was first referenced in 1863, but was probably built shortly after 1853 when the Keeper's Cottage was demolished as part of a refurbishment of this part of the park. The Keeper's Cottage had provided refreshments and this may have been put in place to provide an alternative source of water for visitors. The water would have likely been supplied from the nearby underground reservoir by lead piping.

This fountain is also sometimes unofficially referred to as the Motherstone because of its appearance.

One Tree Hill Conduit Head

This conduit head, on the northern side of One Tree Hill, provided access to the water flowing through a conduit tunnel that starts under Queen Elizabeth's Bower. It is a simple arched opening that is now bricked up and would have also provided access to the conduit for maintenance [Map: E6].

Image 117 One Tree Hill conduit head.

Its curved shape is unusual and it was most likely designed by Nicholas Hawksmoor who was overseeing architectural matters for the Naval Hospital during the upgrading of the water supply at the start of the eighteenth century. The plaque above the arch had an inscription which is now, unfortunately, completely illegible.

If you step up and behind the conduit head you can see the top of the brick conduit that feeds it and which heads off to the south. This conduit is known to continue north east towards Maze Hill and its path is revealed by some manhole covers nearby.

Another conduit house existed in this area, but it was demolished in the nineteenth century.

Image 118: Old conduit in Greenwich Park. PD (no longer extant)

The Vicarage Conduit

Just over the wall behind the boating lake is another conduit house that is now part of the vicarage belonging to St Alfege's Church (The Chantry on Park Vista). The original Tudor brickwork from an outbuilding of the Palace of Pleasaunce is clearly recognisable as it is thinner and more irregular. It is capped by a new tiled roof with an elaborate cross at the apex [Map: D5].

This conduit house would have probably consolidated the water supply from the park and carried it under the original Woolwich Road into the top of the tiltyard where it could have been distributed throughout the palace.

Image 119: Tudor conduit house incorporated into the vicarage.

Snow Well and Stockwell

To the east of Snow Hill, between the road and the Tumuli in a hollow, the remains of a nine metre deep well were discovered. Investigation revealed this was lined with brick with those at the base being from the medieval period indicating that it was much older than the seventeenth century conduits.

The hollow was apparently also used to flog law breakers and a post for that purpose stood here[69]. This well was filled in as it was considered dangerous and its accurate location is currently unknown [Map: G3].

An investigation revealed that, at the bottom, the well opened into a conduit about 1300mm high and 750mm wide that appeared to run down Snow Hill towards St. Mary's gate. This supports the idea that the Snow Well provided water to a public well, the stockwell, that was located behind the herb garden.

---

69   Greenwich Park: Its History and Associations. A. D. Webster,

The stockwell, which gives its name to the nearby street, sold drinking water to the residents of Greenwich. It appears to have also been fed by overflow from the main conduits. When the Naval Hospital upgraded these, the owners petitioned them to ensure they would continue to receive an ample supply of water. In 1732 some of the old conduits were abandoned by the hospital and the stockwell was closed.

Western Admiralty Reservoir

This old reservoir is covered with soil and grass and fenced off as a nature reserve. You are left to wander around its perimeter fence and imagine what is inside beneath the grass [Map: H3].

It was built in 1844 by Sir William Denison to improve the water supply to the Naval Hospital and the Naval Dockyard at Deptford where he was the chief engineer. It is part underground and part above ground. Denison also constructed a reservoir to the east on Shooters Hill to provide water for the Woolwich Dockyard.

With a circumference of over 250 metres and a capacity of five million litres, it is the largest single structure in the park. It was used for 26 years replacing the old supply that dated back to the seventeenth century. When the hospital closed in 1871 and it was no longer used, it was grassed over and screened by trees.

Image 120: Western Admiralty reservoir's uninspiring outside.

It is further south than intended because a well organised protest by the public stopped it being built over the Anglo-Saxon burial mounds, but 12 of the barrows were still destroyed during the preparatory work.

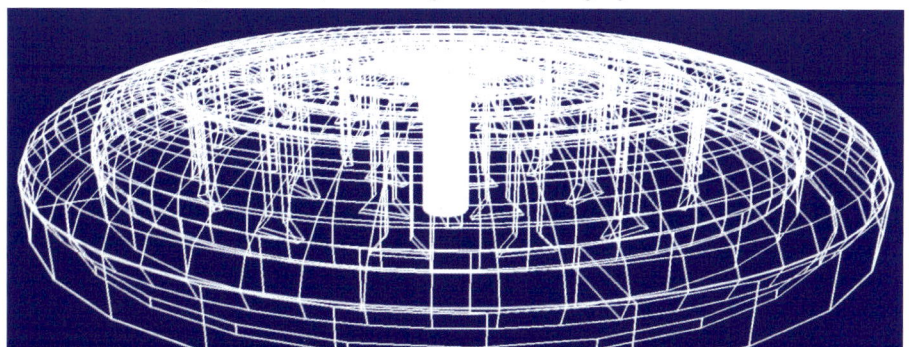

Image 121: A 'blueprint' showing the internal; design of the reservoir.

The interior, impressive as it is, cannot be accessed. It is built of yellow brick as a set of concentric circular arched roofs supported on columns where they join. This creates a large circular space to contain the water with a central column through which access was once provided. There are vents in the roof to allow air into the reservoir.

Image 122: 3D representation of the inside of the Western Admiralty Reservoir.

The Park that Never Was

Since it was fenced in by Humphrey, Duke of Gloucester, the park has been subject to many modifications which have left us with the world heritage site we have today. There are three things that did not happen which would have dramatically altered the park and, arguably, not for the better.

Image 123: How The park might look today had the Le Nôtre designs been implemented. Note the ruins of the old castle where the observatory now is, the cascades flanked by scotch pines leading into a square lake and the grotto hidden in the trees to the left.

The Versailles of London

Had Charles II completed his grand plan for the park, the grassy area in front of the Queen's House would have been a large formal garden full of geometrical lakes, hedges, flower beds and elaborate fountains. The Royal Observatory would probably have been built elsewhere and the palace buildings may well have remained owned by the Crown and only open to the public as paying guests.

The park would not have been such an important amenity and Greenwich would have become a much more well-to-do and less industrial part of London. Greenwich Mean Time would not exist.

Britannia

In 1799, John Flaxman, a classical sculptor and member of the Royal Academy, entered a sketch of a colossal marble statue of Britannia Triumphant in a competition to commemorate Nelson's decisive naval victory over Napoleon Bonaparte at the Battle of the Nile. The statue was to be 80 metres tall and embody British strengths and virtues. It would have stood next to the Royal Observatory dominating the park.

In 1801 he displayed a brass scale model of the statue at the Royal Academy summer exhibition in an attempt to get people to subscribe to its construction, but as sculpture was not in vogue at the time, it attracted little interest.

In 1810 Flaxman became the first Professor of Sculpture at the Royal Academy and the statue was included in the summer exhibition again, but this time with more prominence. The appetite amongst the press and the public for the giant statue remained muted and it was never built.

Image 124 & 125: Britannia Triumphant (right) and how the park might have looked had It been constructed (below)

Railway Viaduct

The railway line that serves Greenwich was the first suburban railway in London. It was completed in 1838 and was carried on 851 brick arches to take it over the roads, predating the underground by several years. It had to terminate at Greenwich because there was no route past the centre of the town and the park.

One approach to solving the problem of extending the line east was a proposal made in 1835 to construct an elaborately decorated viaduct across the park in front of the Queen's House. Although this would have offered fabulous views for the train passengers, for most visitors to the park it would have been a very unwelcome addition.

Drawn on Zinc & Printed by Chapman.

THE PROPOSED GR
as it would appear in Greenwich

G.Landmann.Esqr Engineer.

To allow the railway to proceed eastwards without a viaduct, a shallow cut and cover tunnel was completed in 1878 that runs under the grass between the Queen's House and the Woolwich Road. This required the relocation of a cemetery for seamen that had died in the Naval Hospital. The bodies were moved to East Greenwich Pleasaunce, a small park, where there is a commemorative plaque.

The Royal Observatory failed in a belated attempt to prevent the extension of the railway line as they were concerned that vibrations from the trains would upset their sensitive instruments. Fortunately this did not prove to be the case.

Image 126: One proposal for extending the railway line beyond Greenwich

Trees

Autumn. The tops of beech in the foreground, oak on the left and a cluster of whitebeams centre right. In the background tall London planes

Defined by Trees

More than any London park, Greenwich Park is defined by its trees and the baroque avenues along which almost half of them are found. Unlike the buildings and lawns, the trees provide an ever changing landscape through the seasons with the fresh vibrant blossom of the spring, the lush greens of the summer, the orange and red hues of the autumn and the dark bare branches of the winter, sometimes made magical by a dusting of snow or frost.

It is perhaps because the trees are so integral to the character and nature of the park that they are usually just viewed as part of the background. Indeed, that is almost the aim of the designer: that you should see the avenue, but not the trees. If everything feels natural and in the right place, you will barely notice the design at all.

However, once you see through to the design, you are seeing the history of the park. You have then revealed its structure and the way the trees are used to make each avenue unique. Finally you can pick out some particular trees to admire their elegant shapes and unique features.

Image 127: Trees adding to the winter charm of the park.

An Ever Changing Backdrop

The park contains more than 3,500 trees and over 100 different species[70]. Half of the trees are located along the original seventeenth century avenues and these consist mainly of:

- Spanish Chestnut (Bower Avenue and Great Cross Avenue)
- Horse Chestnut (Blackheath Avenue),
- Lime (The Avenue and Great Cross Avenue)
- Beech and Oak (Jubilee Avenue)
- Hornbeam (Lover's Walk).

This clustering can be seen clearly on the colour-coded map opposite.

Like all living things, trees are forever changing, and since this map is a snapshot from 2014, the park will not be exactly the same as this today. Fortunately trees tend to live to a ripe old age so it is still a good guide.

Comparing a survey made 200 years ago with the modern day we can see how dramatically the tree population has changed. Elm, which once dominated the park, has been devastated by Dutch elm disease and has all but disappeared, replaced by lime and horse chestnut.

Since becoming a public park in 1820, the overall number of trees, and their variety, has increased, especially in the Flower Garden, which has by far the largest selection of trees to be seen in the park.

Tree Type	1812	2014
Elm	1393	10
Chestnut	841	710
Oak	651	463
Fir	42	26
Horse Chestnut	0	379
Lime	0	346
Sycamore	21	113
Beech	6	181

---

70   Royal Parks Tree Survey (2014)

Greenwich Park Trees

- 🟠 Spanish Chestnut (710)
- 🟢 Oak Varieties (463)
- 🔴 Horse Chestnut (379)
- 🟢 Lime (346)
- 🟢 Beech varieties (181)
- 🟤 Cherry varieties
- 🟢 Plane, including London Plane
- 🟡 Sycamore
- 🟦 Hornbeam / Hawthorn / Holly
- 🟢 All other varieties
- ⊙ *Ancient / Older trees (scale)*
- ∘ *Smaller trees (scale)*

Route of original seventeenth century avenues shown in white and overlayed with trees existing in 2014.

Great Trees of London
- Ⓒ Ancient Spanish Chestnut
- Ⓢ Shagbark Hickory

The early morning sun lights up a Norwegian maple. A weather beaten hawthorn in blossom overlooking the Thames

Spanish Chestnut or Sweet Chestnut

Image 128: Two ancient chestnut trees by the observatory during winter when they reveal their age.

Chestnut trees (*castanea sativa*) are not only the most common tree in the park, accounting for one in five, they are also the oldest, with sixty surviving from the great landscaping of the 1660s, each being over 360 years old. The greatest concentrations are on Bower Avenue and on the path between Great Cross Avenue and Croom's Hill gate.

Many of these ancient gnarled specimens were brought from nearby Lesnes Abbey and are easy to spot because of their girth (width). Being deciduous, their age is best observed in the winter months when they are free of leaves. Two fine examples can be seen by the observatory's South Building opposite the Pavilion Tea House and there is a particularly well shaped one close to Maze Hill gate. One, in the Flower Garden, has the accolade of being listed as a 'Great Tree of London'.

Image 129: Mature chestnut bark.

From spring, the chestnut grows clumps of green flowers that have a very strong scent. These develop into an edible nut with a softly spiked husk, which has been a popular ingredient in food dishes all around the world for hundreds of years. The Romans had a liking for them and they adopted the tree from the Greeks who had originally cultivated this species.

The Park Keepers used to farm the chestnuts when the park was private land and took a dim view of anyone foraging or damaging the trees. Today you can gather chestnuts, but only those on the ground.

Image 130: Rose ringed parakeet eating a chestnut.

Sadly the chestnuts are under threat from ink spot disease, oriental gall wasp and sweet chestnut blight. The latter decimated Spanish chestnuts in North America and is increasing in this country, already being present in South East London. It is easily spread by people visiting infected locations and not cleaning their shoes before visiting another.

Chestnut trees typically live 200 to 300 years and reach 20-30m in height. Chestnut timber is not widely used, but is good for furniture and for carving.

That Old Chestnut

Image 131: Spanish chestnut leaves and flowers.

There is nothing boring or repetitive about the old chestnuts in Greenwich Park, despite the expression that takes their name. The phrase 'that old chestnut' is believed to come from a play written in 1808 called The Broken Sword by William Dimond. In it the following dialogue takes place:

Zavillo: ... I entered the wood of Collares, when, suddenly, from the thick boughs of a cork tree...

Pablo: A chestnut, captain, a chestnut!

Zavillo: Bah, you booby! I say a cork!

Pablo: And I swear, a chestnut. Captain. This is the twenty seventh time I have heard you relate this story, and you invariably said a chestnut, till now.

Image 132: Ancient chestnut by Maze Hill gate in June.

Oak

One in every seven trees in the park is an oak, making it the second most common tree. The English oak (*quercus robur*), which is the tree we generally think of as an oak, accounts for most of these, but there are several other varieties. Oaks make up the outer line of the avenues either side of the Queen's House, including Jubilee Avenue, and also the eastern side of the avenue running along the east wall south of Vanbrugh Park gate. They are also common in The Wilderness.

Image 133: Two oaks by Queen Elizabeth's Bower.

There are a few ancient English oak trees and these are to be found on Queen Elizabeth's Bower and on the path from Maze Hill gate towards One Tree Hill.

The oak is considered to be a very English tree and once filled forests across the country. Oaks can live to be well over 500 years old, although 200 to 300 is more typical, and grow to 40m in height.

Oak timber has always been highly prized for its strength and is used in furniture, buildings and boats. Before the advent of steel, the oak tree was a vital resource for the English navy and the trees were often protected by act of parliament. Even the bark is useful, being used in the leather industry for tanning.

Image 134: An ancient oak next to Queen Elizabeth's Bower.

Image 135: Mature English oak with new leaves.

The oak bears a fruit called an acorn, which is not edible by humans, but is very popular with squirrels. Pigs love them too, and in Spain, pigs fed exclusively on acorns, produce the famous Iberian ham with its unique taste.

Image 136: The hairy acorn of the Turkish oak.

The Ultimate Wildlife Hotel

The English oak is capable of supporting over 280 different types of insect and over 700 varieties of lichen, some of which only grow on oak. The branches make good homes for bats and birds, and oak leaves are a popular food for many animals and insects.

The native oak apple is a spherical gall caused by the larvae of a gall wasp, *biorhiza pallida*. It looks

Image 137: A marble oak gall.

like an apple, but is definitely not edible. The marble gall, which was valued in medieval times for making writing ink, is produced by the small brown gall wasp, *andricus kollari*, which was specifically imported into this country to make them. Finally, you may also see a rather grotesque growth like a deformed acorn, and this is another type of gall caused by the wasp, *andricus quercuscalicis*, which appeared in the twentieth century.

Types of Oak

Over the years several new species of oak have been introduced to Britain and are now found in the wild. In the park you will find these varieties.

Species	Number	Distinguishing Features
English Oak	c. 350	Medium sized leaves with five of six rounded lobes. Fissured brown bark. Regular sized acorns.
Turkish Oak	c. 139	Almost identical to English oak with similar leaves, but has large hairy acorns.
Red Oak	c. 23	Oak style leaves turning red in autumn. Has quite large brown acorns.
Holm Oak	c. 38	Holly style leaves and evergreen make this appear unlike an oak, but it develops small green acorns that turn red before dropping.
Spanish Oak	c. 10	Also has holly style leaves, but with small brown acorns.

Drinking Oak

Open a bottle of Rioja, or a New World Chardonnay, and you will be indirectly drinking oak. Oak is a vital ingredient in many wines, both red and white, where storage and ageing in oak barrels significantly modifies the flavour. Oak makes wine less fruity and sweet and introduces vanilla and spicy notes to the taste by adding tannins to the wine. The strength of the 'oaking' is modified by using new, old or even charred barrels, and is an essential part of the vintner's process.

Holm Oak

Introduced to Britain from southern Europe in the fourteenth century, the holm oak (*quercus ilex*) is evergreen and its thick shiny leaves look more like those of a holly. You may rightly wonder why it is classified as an oak, as it does not look like one, but genetically it is very close to the English oak and in the summer you will find it covered in small acorns.

Image 138: Large Holm Oak east of Blackheath Avenue in December.

In the winter it will be one of the few, large, non-conifer trees to keep its leaves. It is also very tolerant to pollution making it ideal as a shade provider in cities.

There is a fine example standing on its own to east of Blackheath Avenue which is quite majestic from a distance. It is even more spectacular if you walk under its canopy where you can inspect its almost black bark and branches.

Like all oaks, its timber is very hard and durable making it useful for all types of construction and carpentry, with the ancient Romans and Greeks using it extensively.

The ancient Greeks revered the oak and believed that the rustling of its leaves in the wind was the voice of Zeus and could foretell the future.

Horse Chestnut

Image 139: Blackheath Avenue with the Horse Chestnuts coming into foliage.

The horse chestnut (*aesculus hippocastanum*) completely dominates Blackheath Avenue where virtually all these trees are to be found, making up about one in nine of the trees in the park. They were all planted in the middle of the last century to replace dead trees. They are also quite common in The Wilderness.

Image 140: Horse chestnut bark, leaves and flowers.

Image 141: Mature horse chestnut on The Avenue.

The horse chestnut is deciduous and its fruit is not edible by humans, or, strangely, even horses, although deer are able to digest them. The nut has a beautiful woody sheen and grows inside a spiky shell which is larger and tougher than that of the chestnut which it resembles. The flowers develop in May and are a pretty white and pink colour.

A horse chestnut tree can live up to 300 years and reach 40m tall. Its timber is not commonly used, but can be suitable for veneer and for turning.

Image 142: Horse chestnut flowers.

Conkers

The fruit of the horse chestnut is known in Britain as a conker and is named after a game called conkers. Conkers are attached to a string so that the players can swing and strike each other's until one breaks and falls off the string. The surviving conker becomes a one-er after its first victory, then a two-er, and so on. The World Conker Championships are still held every year in the village of Southwick in Northamptonshire.

The first games took place in the seventeenth century and used conch shells, hence the name. By the end of the nineteenth century the horse chestnut was the preferred choice for a conker and the game became a seasonal favourite, especially for children.

Image 143: Conkers on Blackheath Avenue.

Lime (or Linden)

Image 144: Lime trees on The Avenue next to St. Mary's gate.

The lime (*tilea europaea*) makes up one in ten of the total park stock. Like the horse chestnut, limes were also planted last century to replace the elm trees which were rapidly being devastated by Dutch elm disease. The lime is probably the most similar of the replacement trees to the elm, and was actually a popular choice for lining avenues at the time when the avenues were first laid out.

Lime trees are to be found lining The Avenue from St. Mary's gate, making up most of the trees as the road continues to the top of Snow Hill. They also form the inner rows on Great Cross Avenue.

Mainly viewed as an ornamental tree, the lime is deciduous, native to Britain, and absolutely no relation to the citrus tree that shares its name. A lime tree lives for 200 to 300 years and achieves a height of 20 to 40 metres. Its timber is light, does not warp and has an almost imperceptible grain making it popular for making musical instruments, toys and small items of joinery. It was the wood of choice for the famous early eighteenth century carver Grinling Gibbons, and examples of his work (in oak) can be seen in St. Alfege's Church.

It has a relatively light and featureless bark and small ovate leaves. In spring it develops small fragrant yellow flowers.

Lime trees have a reputation for covering anything that stands under them for too long with a sticky and hard to remove sap, but do not worry about standing under the trees when you are in the park, as the native limes planted here do not share that undesirable feature which is restricted to those from America.

Image 145: Lime leaves with flowers.

Medicinal Honey

Lime tree flowers have a strong scent in summer that attracts bees. Sleepy or dead bees are often found under the trees and, although this phenomenon is widespread, its cause is unknown. It is suspected that too much pollen might have a toxic effect.

The honey produced from lime trees is highly prized. It is very light coloured, sometimes with a greenish tinge, and has a herbal flavour. It is renowned for being healthy because it is rich in vitamin B1 and also has antiseptic and anti-inflammatory properties. It is especially good for colds and for helping you to get to sleep.

Image 146 Lime bark and new leaves.

Beech

Almost two hundred beech trees (*fagus sylvatica*) can be found in the park with the largest concentration being the inner row of trees on the two avenues either side of the grass parterre in front of the Queen's House. They should feel at home here, since in mythology, they are known as the queen of the trees. Rather romantically, the oak, which makes up the outside rows, is the king of the trees.

Beeches grow well on sandy soil and have been planted in some of the most prominent locations in the park, being found in the courtyard of the observatory, on the side of One Tree Hill and in the Rose Garden. They can easily grow well over 40m high making them one of the tallest native trees in Britain and live for 150 to 200 years.

Image 147: Beech leaves and flowers.

Image 148: Beech leaves and fruits.

The beech produces hardwood timber which is strong, easy to bend and fine grained. It is used in boat building, cabinetry and for flooring. It also burns cleanly and efficiently while generating a lot of heat, making it valued as firewood. Before the advent of fossil fuels it was coppiced specifically for this purpose to support smelting and other industries.

The beech has small ovate leaves which form dense foliage in the summer. In spring it bears small green and brown catkins and by summer these have become small triangular shaped nuts which can be eaten, but are quite bitter.

Beech Books

It is generally accepted that the word book is derived from the Old English word for a beech tree, *boecae*, which was shortened to *boc*. The fact that letters scratched on its smooth grey bark tended to remain for the life of a tree was known to those fond of graffiti way before Roman times and may have influenced its choice as being important for writing.

Image 149: Beech bark.

There were practical reasons too. Wooden writing tablets made from beech had a smooth grain free surface that could easily be inscribed with text. The writing was clear to read and safe from erasure. Being strong and light, sheets of beech could be made thin enough to be bound together to create a wooden book that was not too heavy to carry.

Image 150: A particularly nice beech in the Rose Garden in June.

Image 151: A copper beech on the escarpment near One Tree Hill in spring. The copper beech is ornamental and has been cultivated from the beech.

London Plane

There are almost one hundred London plane trees (*platanus x acerifolia*) distributed throughout the park, but particularly good examples are found on the paths running east from St. Mary's gate. The most noteworthy is the 'One Tree' of One Tree Hill with the seat fitted around it. It has been growing here since 1848 when it replaced another single tree that had been blown down by a storm.

As its name suggests, the London plane is a common tree in London, making up around 8% of all the trees on London streets[71]. They are one of the hardiest trees for planting in towns and a London plane will survive almost anything a city can throw at it, living for 300 years or more and typically reaching 30m in height.

Image 152: The London place tree on One Tree Hill.

---

71 London Tree Survey data 2020. It is second only to the cherry at c.13% of trees.

Image 153: London place leaves.

On streets, where the tree is more stressed, it has a very distinctive smooth mottled bark with a camouflage effect of light and dark greys, but in the park, especially on the older trees, you will only see this in the newer growth.

Image 155: London place fruit and leaves.

Image 154: Typical stressed bark of the London plane.

It is a hybrid tree and produces small round fruits which are inedible. Its timber is used for general construction work and packaging like pallets and crates. It has a close grain and certain cuts create an attractive flecked appearance which can be used for fine carving, when it is sometimes, incorrectly, referred to as 'lacewood'.

A Tree of Mystery and Pedigree

The London plane was 'discovered' in Vauxhall at the start of the seventeenth century by John Tradescant the younger, the son of John Tradescant[72] the elder, who was the gardener to Charles I and Henrietta Maria, among others.

Image 156: John Tradescant the Younger. PD

Both father and son had travelled around the world extensively, seeking out new species of plant to satisfy the craze of having the most exotic garden. However, it seems that the London plane was 'born' in Tradescant's London nursery when two trees he had brought together from opposite sides of the Earth interbred. The London plane is believed to be a hybrid of the American sycamore and the Oriental plane.

By the nineteenth century its tolerance of urban areas meant it had become very popular in towns. Its thin bark peels off easily accounting for the distinctive patterns, but also meaning that pollutants are removed quickly before they can cause harm. Its roots require little space, withstand compaction and its branches can be heavily pruned (or pollarded) without any detrimental consequences.

---

72   John Tradescant 1570-1638 and 1608-1662. The Garden Museum, Lambeth.

Hornbeam

Image 157: Hornbeam trees lining the lower section of Lover's Walk.

Over eighty hornbeams (*carpinus betulus*) can be found on the lower sheltered part of Lover's Walk. A slow growing native deciduous tree, it is highly valued for its extremely strong wood, which is actually the hardest wood from any European tree. It is used for hedging as its slow growth and thick foliage make it ideal for this purpose. It can reach 25m high and live for 300 years.

The hornbeam has an attractive and regular open shape and also works well as part of an avenue where it affords plenty of shade in the summer. It produces catkins and has a fruit that is popular with birds. When mature, its seeds spin as they fall, similar to a sycamore. Its bark is grey and smooth like beech, but has strong vertical lines of alternating darkness.

Good for easily broken teeth

The wood is so dense that it is difficult for carpenters to work with so tends to be used for simple applications that require a very strong simple shape. It is not prone to cracking or splitting and is ideal for making mallets, chopping boards, wooden bowls and even the teeth of the gear wheels found in corn mills.

Even with the advent of iron, wooden gear teeth in the main drive wheel of a windmill were preferred. They resulted in quieter and smoother running and there was also no danger of sparks that could ignite the flour dust. If a sudden gust of wind provided too much power, or the millstone got jammed, the teeth would shear off protecting the windmill from expensive structural damage. The miller could quickly replace the broken teeth and get things running again.

Image 158: Hornbeam bark.

Image 159: Catkins on a hornbeam.

Sycamore

The sycamore tree (*acer pseudoplatanus*) is a member of the plane family and has an attractive and distinctive pink and grey mottled bark. It was introduced to the British Isles in the fourteenth century, possibly by returning crusaders, and has since become naturalised.

It is deciduous and can live for 200 to 400 years, reaching 35m high. With firm and deep roots it can withstand strong winds and so finds use in windbreaks or in any location which is exposed to the elements. Like the London plane, which its bark resembles, the sycamore is very hardy and a good tree for planting in urban areas.

The sycamore has distinctive shiny leaves similar to those of a maple, forming a rounded trident. It has small flowers and these develop into its unusual seeds that have a single wing attached to them so that when they can get caught by wind the seed rotates, keeping it in the air longer, and allowing it to travel further.

The wood is hard and turns yellow with age. It has a fine grain and is easy to work making it ideal for carpentry. It also tends not to stain and so is the perfect wood for making wooden spoons. In Wales, the soft green (unseasoned) wood is viewed as the perfect material for the creation of the famous Welsh love spoon.

Image 160: A fine mature sycamore at the top of Lover's Walk in June.

Image 161: The same sycamore in winter.

Image 162: Sycamore flowers and seeds.

Image 163: Sycamore bark.

A Helicopter

The first British built commercial helicopter was named the Bristol Sycamore, a reference to the spinning of the tree's seeds and their similar shape. It was developed just after the end of the Second World War and was used for both civilian and military purposes, remaining in use by the RAF until 1972.

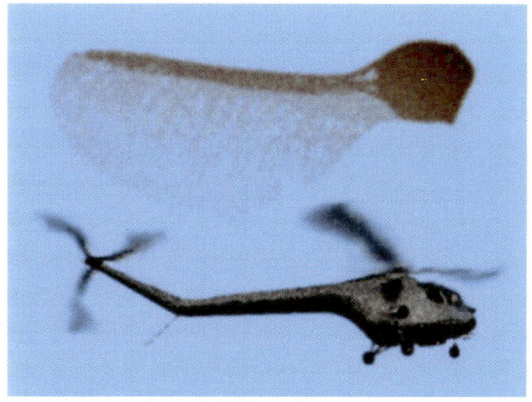

Image 164: Bristol Sycamore.

Cherry

Image 165: Cherry Blossom in April.

There is one path in the park that cannot be missed at the end of April, and that is the path leading from Blackheath Avenue to the Rose Garden. Lined with twenty eight ornamental cherry trees (*prunus serrulata*), the pink blossom is spectacular and extremely popular, especially with visitors from Japan where the tree is known as sakura. The blossom comes out quickly, and fades away equally quickly, so you need to time your visit carefully as it only lasts for two weeks. You will not be alone!

There are another sixty cherry trees spread around the park, generally in clusters to maximise the effect of their blossom. These are mainly ornamental flowering cherry trees, but there are also some wild cherries and these have white blossom. The fruits on these species are small and inedible, but there are other edible fruit trees with blossom, for example you will find apple trees with bright red blossom.

Hanami

Cherry blossom features in the ancient Japanese cultural tradition of Hanami which translates as "view flowers", but is specifically associated with the sakura tree. The sudden blooming of the blossom represents the formation of clouds and symbolises the ever changing and ephemeral qualities of nature. This is a key concept of the Buddhist faith which is the predominant religion in Japan.

The history of Hanami goes back centuries to a time when Japanese farmers saw the blossom as a signal to begin planting their vital rice crops. As the blossom emerged it was believed that the gods, who normally resided in the mountains amongst the clouds, had come down to oversee and bless their new crop, bringing their clouds with them.

Image 166: Traditional Japanese women viewing the cherry blossom. [CC 4.0 rawpixel]

Over time, the celebration became more spiritual, and was adopted by the wealthy and Imperial Court simply to appreciate and enjoy the beauty of nature. As Hanami became an annual festival, it gradually spread throughout the population, where the viewing was often combined with having a meal and drinking sake.

Today it is a major social event in Japan and many other Far Eastern countries. Families and friends gather under the trees to socialise during the day, and often into the night with the help of lanterns suspended in the branches, at which point it is referred to as Yozakura.

Elm

The story of elm trees (*ulmus minor*) in Greenwich Park is a sad one. With just one or two immature, and barely recognisable examples to be found today, it is hard to believe that the elm once made up almost half of the trees in the park. Such has been the devastation wrought by Dutch elm disease caused by a fungus carried by the elm bark beetle.

Image 167: An avenue of elm trees in Peckham Rye park. These trees are Dutch elms rather than English elms.

Not all elms in Britain have succumbed and you can find some on the streets of London and in some other parks where resistant species have been planted.

Some elms do remain in the park, but they are generally not in very good condition and would barely be recognised. New species of elm with some levels of resistance have been cultivated, but they lack the appearance of the original tree.

Image 168: English elm leaves are distinctively asymmetrical at the base as shown here on some new growth on a bush-like tree near Maze Hill gate.

Historical Trees
Queen Elizabeth's Oak

Image 169: Queen Elizabeth's Oak. Now a five star hotel for insects and mini-beasts.

When the park was landscaped for James I and Charles II with a systematic replanting, this tree was already four hundred years old. It survived two hundred further years until, at the end of the nineteenth century, it died of old age. The dead tree continued to stand firmly upright for a further one hundred years covered in a thick layer of Ivy.

By the time it died its trunk had a girth of almost seven metres and the internal cavity, which was paved, had a seat around the sides that could comfortably seat fifteen people. It had a door fitted to the entrance and a window was made in the side that looked out over One Tree Hill.

Image 170: Queen Elizabeth's Oak with One Tree Hill in the background. [c.1905 Postcard] PD

It is not known exactly how old the tree is but an analysis of its ring structure indicates that it started growing around 1300[73]. It was already two hundred years old by the time Henry VIII and Elizabeth I were at Greenwich and one of the most significant features of the park.

It was recorded that in 1519, Henry VIII and Anne Boleyn, danced around this tree during their courtship [Map: G5]. It Is also likely that it was beneath this tree that Henry VIII sat contemplatively to listen for the guns which, by his command, were to be fired when Anne Boleyn was beheaded[74].

As a girl growing up in Greenwich, Elizabeth I loved the park. This oak was named after her because during her walks she was said to have taken refreshments inside the tree where she was protected from the elements, as even then, the tree was hollow.

Queen Elizabeth's Oak was enclosed within the walls of the grounds of the Keeper's Cottage when it was built and this helped protect it. The base of a water pump and animal drinking trough that were used by the Keeper's Cottage can be found in the vicinity.

Until the demolition of the Keeper's Cottage in 1853, the tree was still being used by visitors to take refreshments. They were able to purchase a cup of tea or some fruit from the orchard. A.D. Webster, the park superintendent, recalls that it was also used as a kiosk to pay the park workmen around that time and that some people were temporarily detained within the tree after breaking the branches of the chestnut trees while taking the nuts.

There would have originally been many oak trees in the area, but so many were cut down for their timber to be used in building work or to construct men-of-war for the Tudor navy, that ancient oaks are today quite rare. Being within the Keeper's Cottage grounds, Queen Elizabeth's Oak was also safe from the French landscape gardeners who had no place for oak trees in their formal designs, although the park keeper would have probably used the acorns as pig feed.

---

73 Dr Jane Sidell, English Heritage.
74 Contemporary accounts imply he was hunting in Epping, but modern evidence suggests this was unlikely.

On October 15th 1987, a devastating storm struck the country. Four hundred trees were brought down in the park, but even though Queen Elizabeth's Oak had been dead for over 100 years, it was so substantial that even this storm was not enough to fell it.

Image 171: Queen Elizabeth's Oak not long before it fell.

However, it was damaged, and despite some work to strengthen the remains with steel reinforcements, another storm on January 25th 1990, proved to be too much for it.

Today the gradually decaying remains of the original tree are enclosed by railings along with a new oak planted in December 1992 by the Duke of Edinburgh. He was also Baron Greenwich, and had strong associations with the town, especially the Cutty Sark.

Opposite it, behind a small stone plaque hidden in the grass, is an oak planted in 1977 to celebrate the silver jubilee of Queen Elizabeth II.

Great Trees of London

Greenwich Park contains two of the Great Trees of London[75], a list consisting of around fifty trees selected by public vote and which all have a strong physical character, are of historical importance and form a key part of a landscape. Both of these trees are in the Flower Garden.

Spanish Chestnut (*castanea cativa*)

Just one of the historic ancient Spanish chestnut trees has been given the honour of being a Great Tree of London and it can be found in the Flower Garden just inside the Vanbrugh gate.

---
75   https://en.wikipedia.org/wiki/Great_Trees_of_London

Having been very well looked after over the centuries it is an excellent specimen of its type, has a massive trunk and has had some of its taller branches removed to maintain its health and stability as well as facilitate anti-aircraft fire during World War II.

As the Spanish chestnut has already been covered elsewhere, the only thing to add is that if you are visiting this tree in autumn you may be able to collect some of its edible nuts. Do make sure to only take windfalls rather than risk damaging this historic tree. If you find some then hopefully you will enjoy them as much as those who eat them over 300 years ago.

Shagbark Hickory (carya ovata)

This tree is a native of North America and stands on the left of the path from the lake to the Flower Garden.

It is a large deciduous tree that can easily grow to be more than 30m tall and is a member of the hickory family. It produces an edible sweet fruit, the hickory nut, which looks like a chestnut but without the spines. The sap is edible too and can be tapped to produce a syrup in a similar way to the maple tree.

It has a distinctive bark which you may not consider justifies its name, but the bark of this particular tree is not as "shaggy" as it can get, where long thin flakes attached at the top give the appearance of the trunk being covered in giant course hairs.

Shagbark hickories were brought to Britain around 1629 and proved to be very suited to the climate. Its hickory nuts are considered to be some of the finest in the world and comparable to pecans, but although they were very popular in America, they never became popular in Britain and so the trees remained a rare curiosity despite their potential.

Image 172: Shagbark hickory fruits.

Image 174: How shaggy is this bark? Not as shaggy as normal!

Image 173: Leaves and flowers of the Shagbark Hickory in May.

Hickory is a fine grained hardwood and is associated with making hockey sticks and other sporting equipment.

The shagbark hickory.

Other Noteworthy Trees
Himalayan Cedar

Image 175: Himalayan cedar close to the Knife Edge statue.

The Himalayan cedar (*cedrus deodara*) is found throughout the park providing a splash of green throughout the year with its attractive sweeping and drooping branches that form a spectacular canopy. This is especially so in the flower garden where there are several trees and they create a natural hiding place for young children to explore.

Like most conifers it has needle-like leaves and produces cones, the large cones being female (seed carrying) and the small ones male (pollen carrying). It is a hardy tree and can live for over 500 years, although 200 is more normal.

In this country the tree is entirely ornamental and popular because of its gracious appearance, however, in its native habitat of the southern Himalaya, its wood is heavily used in construction, especially as it is naturally resistant to rot.

Its timber is soft and broad grained making it unsuitable for fine work, but the oils that make it resistant to rotting and unpopular with insects, are also extracted to make incense and essential oils. Being so useful and looking so good, it is not surprising to find that it is the national tree of Pakistan.

Image 176: A proliferation of large cones on a Himalayan cedar.

Scots Pine

The Scots pine (*pinus sylvestris*) is the only truly native pine tree in the British Isles and, despite its name, originated in Southern England at the end of the last ice age before spreading north as the climate warmed and the broad leaved deciduous trees crowded them out. It came to make up a large part of the native forests in Scotland where it was too cold for deciduous trees, thereby acquiring its name. It is actually found throughout the northern hemisphere and is the most common species of pine tree in the world.

Image 177: A Scots pine on the escarpment just to the east of the observatory.

Scots pine were planted in Greenwich Park during the great landscaping to form a dramatic boundary either side of the terraced steps.

The Scots pine has a tall, straight reddish brown trunk that is usually clearly visible through the foliage which is finer and sparser than most other conifers. It provides a typical softwood timber, but is characterised by large knots which make it better suited to construction than carpentry. It is still a very important timber plantation tree and they can typically live for 200 to 300 years growing to 20 to 30 metres.

Image 178: Scots pine young cones. *Image 179: Bark of the Scots pine.*

Christmas

The Scots pine is not a particularly popular Christmas tree in the United Kingdom despite it being Britain's only native conifer. It has strong branches, does not drop its needles and, because the wood is rich in oil, it generates a strong woodland fragrance. They are very hard to find so if you want one for Christmas in a few years the best thing to do is plant one now!

Giant Sequoia Sapling

When we think of really large trees, we often reference the great American redwoods, in particular the giant sequoia (*sequoiadendron giganteum*).

These incredibly lofty trees often have an enormous girth and in California they can grow to be 80m tall and have a diameter of 10m at the base of their trunk. They can also live to be as much as 3,000 years old.

However, all trees have to start somewhere, and this young giant sequoia is interesting for that reason, especially as saplings of this species exhibit a somewhat strange and characteristic elongated conical trunk, somewhat like an inverted ice cream cone.

You will need to move around it to get a good impression of its red trunk through the gaps in its foliage and then use your imagination to picture it in a hundred years or so when it will probably be the tallest tree in the park.

Image 180: Sequoia sapling.

Image 181: Mature sequoia in Sussex.

Hawthorn

The hawthorn (*crataegus*) is commonly associated with hedges as it is extremely hardy, small and its thorns deter animals from trying to break through. The boundary hedge south of the playground contains hawthorn.

Hawthorn is not a naturally large tree, but allowed to grow on their own, they can reach 5

Image 182: Ancient Hawthorn next to the Maze Hill gate.

Image 183: Hawthorn blossom.

Figure 184: Haws.

to 15m in height and live for 150 years. The leaves are oak-like but more triangular in shape. Because it flowers in May, it is also known as the May tree.

The hawthorn is steeped in mythology being referenced in both folklore and religion. On the one hand the blossom is associated with fertility, with the flowers being used as bridal garlands. On the other, it is considered extremely unlucky to bring hawthorn blossom into the house as it will lead to illness.

The flowers are most commonly white, but some varieties have pink or red blooms and both can be seen in the park. The hawthorn develops a small red fruit called the haw which is a shiny red and should not be eaten raw. In the past it was used to make wine and jellies.

Silver Birch

Image 185: A cluster of silver birches at the south east corner of the parterre. The red in the grass is sheep sorrel, a plant that loves acid grassland.

The silver birch (*betula pendula*) is an elegant tree and instantly recognisable by its distinctive flaky silver bark with pronounced black markings. It has triangular leaves and long delicate catkins which produce a mass of fine seeds which are distributed by the wind.

It is not ideally suited to the British climate and rarely reaches its normal 15 to 20m height. It is also fairly short lived, typically living for 50 to 70 years. Its strong and heavy timber was perfect for making bobbins for the cotton industry which required thin stems that could be grown rapidly through coppicing.

The silver birch is the national tree of Finland where a bunch of leafy young branches is used as a 'vinta' in a sauna to beat the skin and improve blood circulation and thereby enhance the therapeutic effect of the heat.

Image 186: Silver birch are at their most elegant when they are young.

Image 187: Bark, catkins and leaves.

Tulip Tree

Image 188: Tulip Trees in the Flower Garden.

The tulip tree (*liriodendron tulipifera*) is a member of the magnolia family and a native of North America. It is so named because it bears flowers that resemble a tulip, but unlike the magnolia which flowers in April, the tulip tree does not flower until June. The flowers are quite robust with long yellow stamen. They typically have a pale green and yellow colour with a red/orange marking around the base. The tulip tree has very characteristic chunky leaves with four lobes.

It is deciduous, hardy and long lived, being capable of reaching over 40m in height. Consequently it is a popular choice in many ornamental gardens and there are three fine examples in the Flower Garden.

Image 189: Flowers on a tulip tree.

Ginkgo

The ginkgo tree (g*inkgo biloba*) is close to the tulip trees and is noted for its unusual fan shaped leaves. It originates from China and its main claim to fame is that it is a 'living fossil' in that it has hardly changed in appearance for almost 200 million years. Dinosaurs would have roamed past trees just like this one.

Image 190: Ginkgo leaves.

A Hollow Oak and a Dead Oak

The Wilderness provides a small but pleasant semi-wild woodland area in the park where, as well as looking at the deer, you can spot birds and wildlife. It is left to appear as natural as possible with dead and fallen trees encouraging insect life. Children are able to play games here that are a little closer to nature, although the main playground still seems far more attractive.

Image 191: Dead oak with an ivy covering and a hollow oak.

Queen Elizabeth's Oak may have fallen some years ago, but hiding in this area are two old oak trees that represent scaled down versions of Queen Elizabeth's Oak during its long life. One is a tree with a hollowed out trunk, albeit barely able to seat fifteen fairies, let alone fifteen people, and the other is a dead tree surrounded and supported by Ivy.

Planted Areas

The majority of the garden features in the park were added during the twentieth century and provide points of horticultural interest as well as a splash of colour.

The Flower Garden

This is by far the largest planted area in the park and has several circular beds stocked from March through to November. It also has the largest variety of trees. It is fenced off from the rest of the park with four entrance gates and dogs are not allowed in. With its pleasant lawns and shady trees it is an ideal place for a picnic [Map: K6].

The southernmost section is fenced off and kept wild as it is the deer park. Originally this area was called the Great Wilderness and was planted in the 17th century to provide wood for the royal palace. It was divided into eleven rectangular plots separated by wide access routes and is now known simply as The Wilderness.

A further four plots were added in the south west corner and called the Little Wilderness. That area is now The Dell and American Garden.

In 1854 work began to create an ornamental garden, including the construction of the nurseries which occupy the south east corner of the park and provide all the storage for the park maintenance equipment.

While this planting was going on, the deer were still free to roam through the whole park and the new plants, with their tasty shoots, needed to be protected from being eaten with individual fencing. Lawns were laid, flower beds created and ornamental trees planted.

One of the last features to be installed was the lake which was intended to be a showcase for aquatic and other water loving plants. Instead it has become a home for all sorts of waterfowl as the water quality has proved hard to manage [Map K5].

Image 192: The lake and a cormorant.

By 1898 the Flower Garden had been fenced off from the rest of the park with the boundary it has today. The extensive planting continued until 1900 at which time such elaborate gardens were unique for a public park.

The Gardener's Chronicle was impressed and in 1925 wrote of Greenwich Park: "The greatest attraction from a gardening point of view in the enclosed part known as the Flower Garden. This pleasure ground is arranged quite differently to that commonly adopted in public parks, one would imagine oneself to be in the midst of a beautiful garden attached to some stately home".

This is undoubtedly still true today.

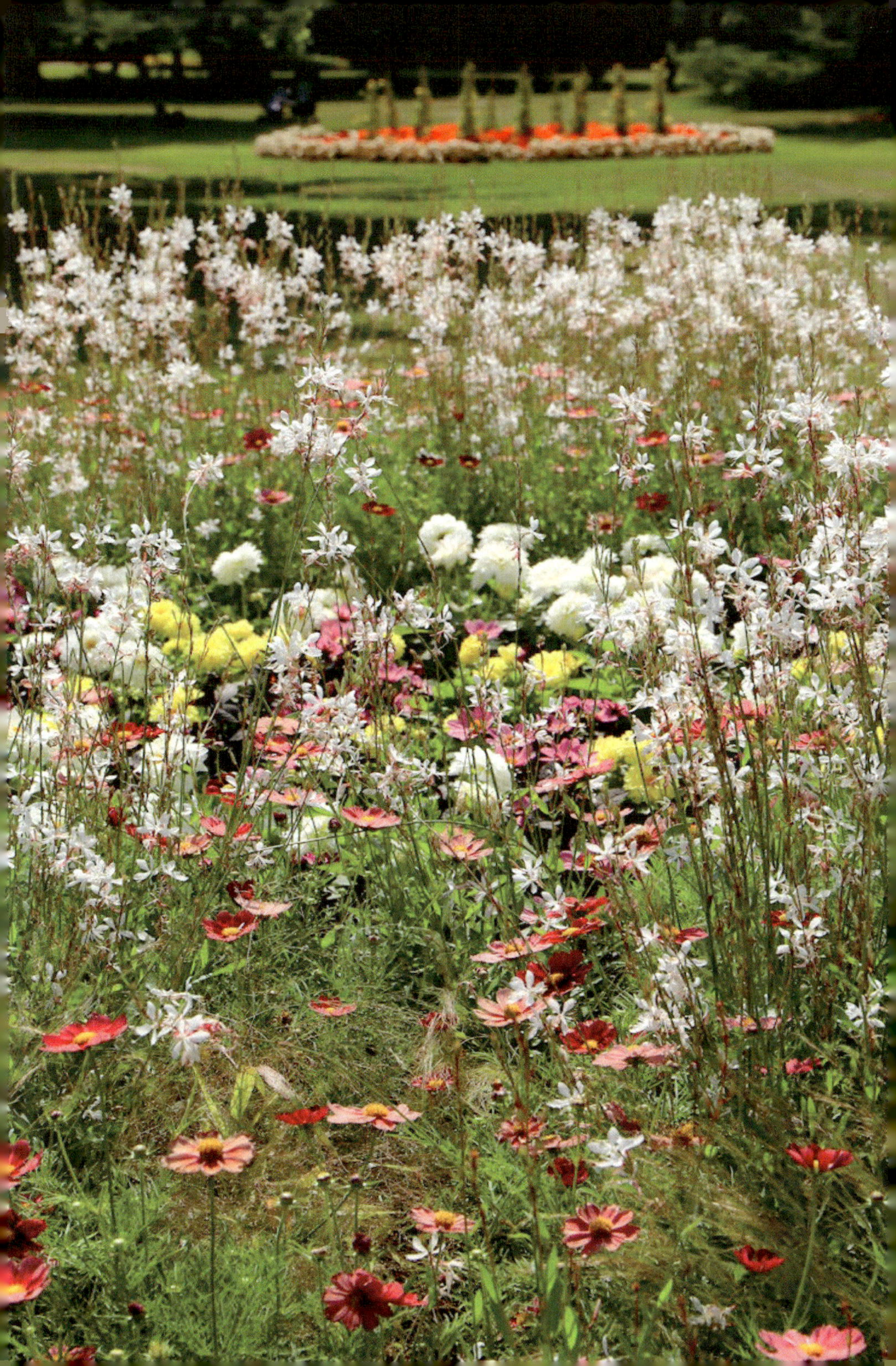

Rose Garden

Overlooked by the Ranger's House, with its own gate in the wall, the rose garden was laid-out in the sixties and is a very seasonal part of the park, at its best in June and July [Map: J2].

A board by the southern entrance shows which roses are being grown in each bed, but some of the roses are having to be replaced as they are old and unhealthy. Wild flower beds have been planted to allow the soil to recover and these provide a very different and extremely colourful way to fill the gaps.

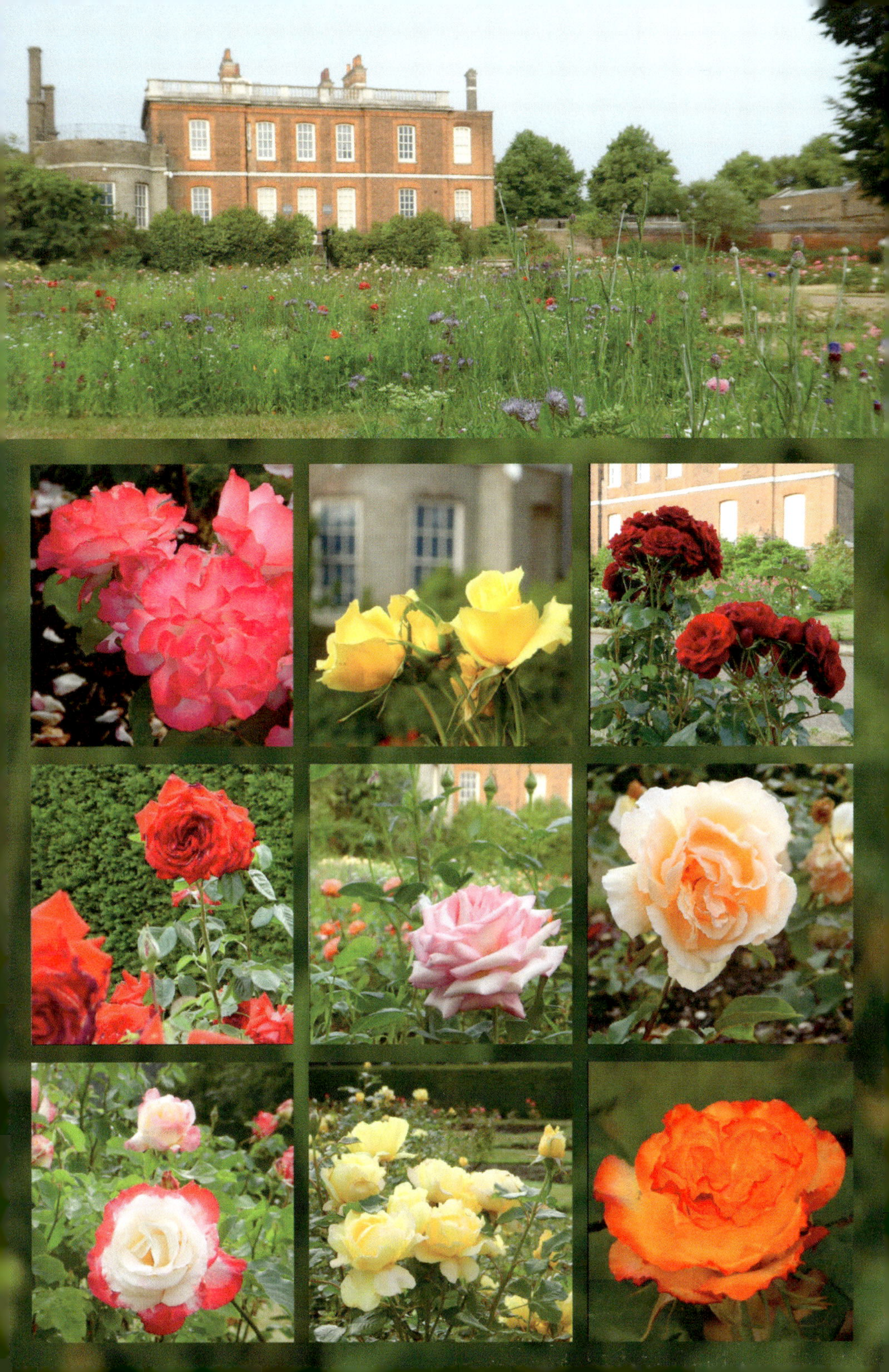

The Herb Garden

Redesigned in 1990, the quiet herb garden is found just west of St Mary's gate [Map: E2]. With its central fountain designed by Kate Malone and installed in 2000 to celebrate the millennium, it is reminiscent of an abbey cloister's garth, or garden.

Image 193: The Herb Garden showing the central fountain and herb beds.

Monks grew herbs for flavouring their food and ale, as well as for their medicinal properties. Herbs were grown in Greenwich Park for very similar reasons by the Naval Hospital who would have used them in cooking and to alleviate any mild ailments of their inmates.

The extensive range of herbs and their locations can be seen below.

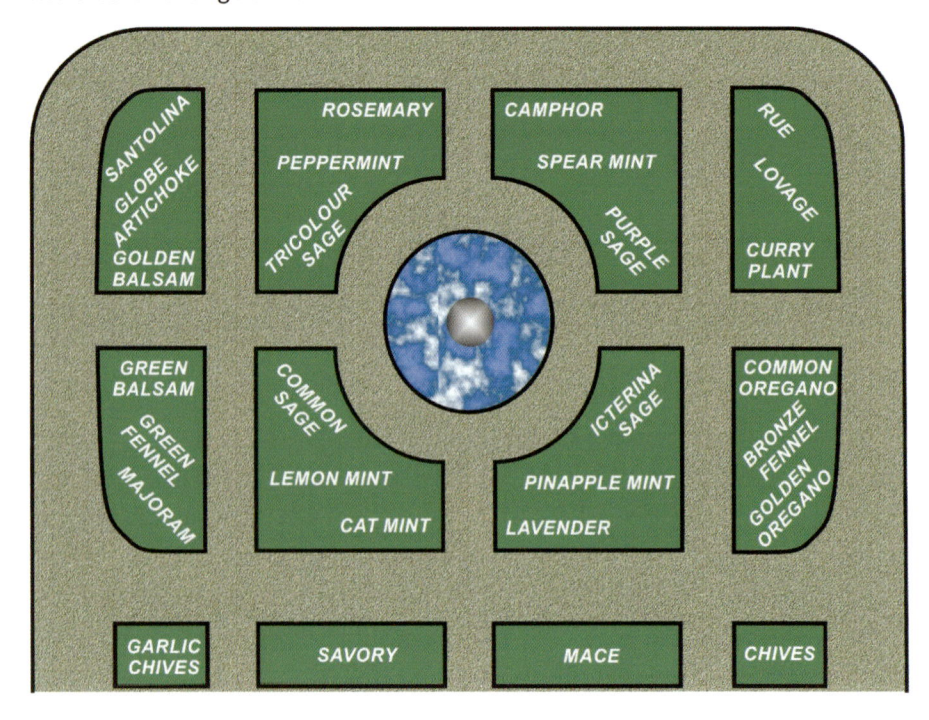

Top row	SANTOLINA, GLOBE ARTICHOKE, GOLDEN BALSAM, ROSEMARY, PEPPERMINT, TRICOLOUR SAGE, CAMPHOR, SPEAR MINT, PURPLE SAGE, RUE, LOVAGE, CURRY PLANT
Middle row	GREEN BALSAM, GREEN FENNEL, MAJORAM, COMMON SAGE, LEMON MINT, CAT MINT, ICTERINA SAGE, PINAPPLE MINT, LAVENDER, COMMON OREGANO, BRONZE FENNEL, GOLDEN OREGANO
Bottom row	GARLIC CHIVES, SAVORY, MACE, CHIVES

Herb information

This short list describes how the herbs in this garden were, and are, used.

Bronze Fennel
Grown for its seeds, not its bulb. Treats colic in babies and found in gripe water.

Camphor – Not Edible
Mainly medicinal and used to treat pain, burns and coughing.

Catmint
Used to make herbal tea. Treats an upset stomach, diarrhoea and nausea.

Chives
A mild onion flavour for cooking, rich in antioxidants and reduces inflammations.

Common oregano
A flavouring often used with tomato and found on pizza. Treats skin related problems.

Common sage
A distinctive seasoning for poultry and treats digestive problems inducing flatulence.

Curry plant
A spicy flavouring for rice and potato dishes. Acts as an expectorant.

Globe artichoke
Eat as a vegetable. Reduces nausea and inflammation.

Golden balsam – Not edible.
Used to treat warts and burns as well as rheumatism and other joint pains.

Golden oregano
Similar to common oregano.

Green balsam – Not edible.
Antiseptic properties as a paste.

Green fennel
Mainly used for cooking with its large edible bulb and foliage providing a mild aniseed taste.

Garlic chives
Flat leaves used in cooking to impart a garlic flavour.

Icterina sage
Similar to sage, but with yellow and green variegated foliage.

Lavender
Its strong smell relaxes and reduces anxiety. It can also flavour food in small amounts.

Lemon mint
Similar to spearmint, but imparts a lemon tang to food. Good for oral infections.

Lovage
A type of parsley, used to flavour stews and soups. Good for the digestion.

Mace
Imparts a mild flavour to stews and salads. The dried foliage repels insects. Note the Asian spice mace is made from nutmegs.

Marjoram
A sweeter alternative to sage. Good for colds and digestive disorders.

Peppermint
Has a strong mint flavour when eaten. Good for treating digestive problems.

Pineapple mint
A mild mint flavour, otherwise similar to spearmint.

Purple sage
Similar to sage, but with a purple colouration

Rosemary
Favours meat, fish and breads. Relieves muscle pain and improves the memory.

Rue
With a distinctive and strong aroma it is often used to flavour East African cuisine.

Santolina
An unusual flavour used in stews and soups. Has insect repellent properties.

Savory
The 'herb of love' and reputedly an aphrodisiac. Treats digestive ailments.

Spearmint
An excellent herbal tea. Used in salads and sauces, especially for lamb and chicken.

Tricolour sage
A polychromatic version of sage.

The Queen's House Herbaceous Border

Image 194: The Herbaceous Border.

Running for about 180m from Jubilee Avenue to Park Row gate, this Herbaceous Border is the longest in London, if not the whole of Britain [Map: D4]. Although first planted out in 1925, it was not until 1950, long after the deer were no longer free to enjoy feeding on the gardeners' hard work, that it became the beautiful feature it is today.

Queen's Orchard

This section of the park is enclosed behind the park wall and accessed through an attractive decorative wrought iron gate by the Creed Place entrance next to the playground. As it is staffed by volunteers, it is only open at specific times so check these before visiting [Map: D6].

The area was first recorded in 1693 as one of three dwarf orchards planted for the Queen's House. When the Naval Hospital was founded, the land was taken from the park and eventually passed to Greenwich Council where it was used for allotments during the Second World War. It returned to the ownership of the Royal Parks in 2011 and the new garden was created and opened to the public on 15th April 2013.

It is now a well established gardener's garden with an ornamental pond, a wildlife pond, several raised vegetable beds and an orchard of fruit trees. The fruit trees are old varieties that date back to Tudor times and include apples, pears, cherries, medlar[76] and quince. Just through the gate is a dry well with an ornamental cover by Heather Burrell, who also designed the gate.

Image 195: The Queen's Orchard with the well in the foreground and ancient fruit trees to the back.

Image 196: Queen's Orchard vegetable beds.

---

76 Medlar, is a small tree bearing a fruit of the same name. Cultivated since Roman times, it is unusual in that the fruit can be harvested in winter, and needs to be over-ripened, or bletted, before they can be eaten.

The Wilderness and Deer

Image 197: Red and fallow deer relaxing in the park.

At the south eastern end of the park is The Wilderness, a fenced off area for the deer [Map K6], that once roamed the entire park.

Edward IV is the first person to be recorded as hunting deer in the park[77], probably a self-sustaining colony that had been fenced in by Humphrey, Duke of Gloucester. Henry VIII began buying deer to restock the park and, in 1510, barely a year on the throne, he paid a Eustace Browne £13 for more deer. This continued, with deer regularly being brought to Greenwich Park, often from the palace at Eltham.

When the park was landscaped in the seventeenth century the deer were actually excluded from Great Wilderness as it was set aside for growing new trees and the deer would have eaten them.

By the late eighteenth century the deer were purely ornamental and, without hunting to keep down the numbers, the head keeper reported that they were not in very good condition. During very busy times. such as public holidays and

---

77 Old and New London: Volume 6, Cassell, Petter & Galpin

fair days, when the park was full of boisterous people, the deer were rounded up and kept in The Wilderness to protect them[78].

At the start of the twentieth century there were 150 deer throughout the park and the deer enclosure in The Wilderness was used to assist with fawning and feeding. A.D. Webster, superintendent of the park, recorded that when the park closed in the evening, the deer would seek out scraps left by visitors even when the grass was at its most luscious, often making them ill, sometimes fatally.

The mixture of deer and people was also problematic for visitors, with several reports of deer attacking people who came too close and, in 1906, a man was killed by a buck[79]. By 1927 traffic was running through the park and the deer were considered to be a danger to both the vehicles and themselves. It was decided to cull the herd and restrict the remaining deer to the enclosure in The Wilderness.

Today there are around thirty deer consisting of a mixture of red deer and fallow deer. There are two designated viewing areas where you can observe them. The best time is early morning or evening as this is when they are most active.

Figure 198: A red deer calf in The Wilderness.

78 Greenwich Park Conservation Plan 2019-2029
79 Kentish Mercury, 5th April 1906

Identifying the deer

The red deer are the larger animals with a dark reddish-brown coat while the fallow deer are smaller with a lighter brown coat with white spots. Only the males have antlers. The females have a similar coat to the males, but are smaller.

Red Deer
Red brown coat, little mottling.
1.2m high at shoulders.
Stick like antler with many branches.
Uncharacteristic rump.

Fallow Deer
Pale brown coat, white mottling.
0.8m high at shoulders.
Spade like antlers (palmate).
Distinctive black and white rump.

Red Deer

Red deer (*cervus elaphus*) are native to Britain, being the largest British mammal. They prefer to live in forests, but as these were felled by early man, they declined in numbers, until the Normans began to keep them in parks for hunting.

Image 199: Red Deer in Greenwich Park in early December.

Their characteristic red coat is brightest in the summer, thickening and darkening for the winter months. The males, or stags, typically weigh around 200kg and are 1.3m high at the shoulders. The stags are easy to spot because they are much larger than the females, or hinds, and are the only ones to sport antlers. The antlers are shed and regrown each year in the spring.

In their natural forest habitat red deer are solitary animals with groups tending to be mothers and their calves, but in captivity and open space they tend to congregate in single sex groups. The rutting (or breeding) season occurs between September and October, taking place at dawn or late evening when the stags seek to attract the females by roaring, strutting and exerting their dominance over the other males, sometimes with a violent clash of antlers that can lead to injury. Once a stag has gained his authority, he has to remain alert and protect his harem from mating attempts by the other males.

The hinds give birth after eight months in May and June and the calf is able to join the herd after two weeks and fully support itself after two months. During this time the hinds can be heard mooing when the young wander too far. The calves are born spotted and a few spots may even be retained into early adulthood. To avoid confusing the young red deer with fallow deer, it is important to note the colour of the coat as well as the presence of spots.

Red deer typically live for twenty years in captivity, with the stags mating once they reach four or five.

Image 200: Stag growing new antlers.

Fallow Deer

Image 201: Fallow Deer showing their spade antlers and distinctive rump.

Fallow deer (*dama dama*) are native to Europe, but not Britain, where they were brought during the Roman period. They were kept in parks and became naturalised in British forests as they escaped. They prefer to eat grass, but also eat the shoots of trees and shrubs.

They have several coat types, but the breed in the park has a light brown coat with a white mottled pattern which becomes more grey and indistinct during the winter months. Their rumps are usually white with a black border and relatively long black and white striped tail. Only the adult males (bucks) have antlers and fallow deer are the only species in Britain where they are spade shaped. As with red deer, the antlers are lost and regrown in the spring. The males are typically 100kg in weight and 0.8m high at the shoulders with the females (does) being significantly smaller.

Fallow deer normally live in single sex groups, only coming together during their rutting season which starts mid-October. The dominant males assert their authority over each other, often with loud groaning and the clashing of antlers. In the wild, mating is instigated by the females visiting a territory marked out by the males for that purpose, called a lek and referred to as lekking, but some deer, especially those in captivity, adopt the harem approach.

The young (fawns) are born after eight months in June and July. They are completely dependent on their mother for the first two weeks and can follow the herd after four. A year old fawn is fully independent, but the bucks do not grow antlers until they are three or four. They typically live to be sixteen in captivity.

Wildlife

Like most urban parks, Greenwich Park is not a great haven for wildlife. Firstly it is surrounded by a wall so that even the most intrepid visitors, like foxes and mice, are only able to get in through the same gates as people. Secondly it is very busy and popular with dog walkers whose charges often enjoy chasing something. It does, however, have three reserves for wildlife: The Wilderness, the Western Admiralty Reservoir and the escarpment under the observatory.

Grey Squirrels

Grey Squirrels are the only 'wild' animals you are likely to see because for them the wall around the park presents no barrier and dogs cannot climb trees. Through feeding, many have become quite tame and run towards people expecting food, rather than running away.

Image 202: On One Tree Hill, two squirrels on a branch, while Canary Wharf is shrouded in mist.

They are not popular with the park management because of the damage they do to the trees by gnawing through the bark to get at the sweet sap underneath. If this is done excessively it can very easily kill part of a tree, or even the whole tree. Even if the tree survives, the removal of the bark creates a wound that weakens it and makes it much more susceptible to other infections or pests.

Foxes

Urban foxes are very common in London and some have chosen to build their dens in the park in a quiet area. Generally they do not like big open spaces or dogs, so you will be most likely to see one early in the morning in the flower garden or The Wilderness amongst the deer. Feeding by visitors has made some quite fearless of people and a nuisance.

Image 203: A fox roaming through The Wilderness.

In London, foxes generally prefer to live along the railways which give them long safe corridors through which to travel. They do like human food scraps and you should avoid putting edible items in the park bins as the foxes are likely to pull all the rubbish out to get to the food.

Wood mice and other small mammals

The Wilderness and other areas where the public do not have general access, are perfect habitats for wood mice and other small mammals which tend not to travel far from their nests. It is unlikely that you will see them unless you are on an organised tour as they are primarily nocturnal and keep well away from people.

Birds

With so many trees, it is hardly surprising that Greenwich Park is home to plenty of birds, but they are too often heard, but not seen. Ducks, geese, pigeons, crows and robins are the exceptions to this rule. Since recording began in 1850, over 150 different species have been observed in the park. Here are some that you might see on a typical stroll, but to maximise your chances go early morning on a nice day. All the pictures without a red dot were taken in the park.

Very common

You will have had your eyes shut if you don't see any of these.

Carrion Crow
Magpie
Robin
Rose ringed parakeet
Wood Pigeon

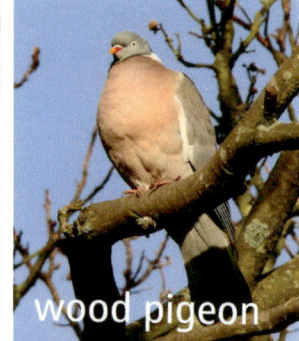

Sometimes seen

If you are having a longer walk in the wooded areas and are actively looking for birds then you should see at least some of these, especially in The Wilderness and Flower Garden.

Blackbird, Blue Tit, Goldfinch, Great Tit, Jackdaw, Jay, Long Tailed Tit, Sparrow, Wren

Lucky break

These are pretty hard to come by, but can be found around the park:

Black Cap
Chaffinch
Chiff Chaff
Coal Tit
Great Spotted Woodpecker
Green Finch
Green Woodpecker
Mistle Thrush
Pied Wagtail
Song Thrush

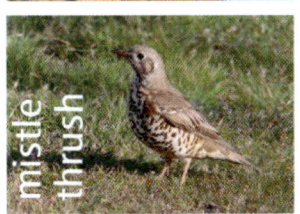

Insects

The park is full of insects which is scarcely surprising as a single tree can support hundreds of different species. Crickets, spiders and beetles can be hunted for, but the flying ones, including butterflies, dragon flies and bees are much more easily seen.

Of those on the ground, then it is the stag beetle that you should be looking out for, as although relatively rare, they are less so in South London. They are very large, reaching up to 75mm in length, and congregate around decaying wood.

About a dozen types of butterfly can be seen, mainly on hot, sunny days. Some, like the cabbage white and meadow brown, prefer areas of long grass, while others are attracted to flowers in the many planted areas. Dragonflies can also be found on the grasslands or by the lake.

Perhaps the most interesting insects are those that take advantage of the acid grassland and burrow in the soil. Of these the most important are the mining bees and wasps.

Image 205: Comma and meadow brown.

Mining bees are solitary bees and do not form communal nests. Instead the female bee digs a burrow in firm sand or sandy soil leaving a bee sized hole surrounded by a small mound in the ground. It is this type of bee or wasp that would live in an 'insect hotel'. Some bees, like the rather loud green-eyed flower bee (anthophora bimaculata), create many individual burrows crowded into one favourable area, usually south facing. Others dig a longer burrow and add small chambers in the sides where the eggs can be laid along with nectar.

Once the nectar is stored and eggs aid, the hole is covered and left. When the eggs hatch, the larvae eat the nectar and then pupate, over wintering and emerging as adult bees the following year.

Image 206: A little flower bee approaches her nest on the escarpment.

Little flower bees are at their most active in the summer when they are collecting pollen from the flowers to put in their nest. Other species of mining bee, such as the tawny mining bee are seen earlier in the year.

You may notice some iridescent insects searching and scratching among the holes that the mining bees have dug. These are cuckoo wasps, and like their avian namesake, they lay their eggs in the bees nest. When they hatch they eat the nectar and bee larvae.

Image 207: Jewel or cuckoo wasp.

The bee wolf is even more gruesome. This wasp captures and paralyses honey bees which it then places in its nest as food for its larvae to feed on. It tends to produce long burrows with several hatching chambers.

Image 208: The bee wolf wasp.

2012 Olympics

In July and August 2012 Greenwich Park was closed to the public as it was staging the equestrian events of the 2012 London Olympic Games. The park was also closed during July in 2011 to stage test events.

Image 209: Olympic test event July 2011.

The park became almost unrecognisable with the area in front of the Queen's House being converted into a huge temporary stadium for dressage, jumping and

Image 210: The dressage grand prix special competition. (c) Lvaughn7 CC BY-SA 4.0.

eventing. The cross-country section of the eventing included a course that used almost every corner of the park.

The Queen's House was used by the Olympic organising committee as one of their offices and following the Olympics it was refurbished and became an art gallery for the Maritime Museum's collection.

The extent of the changes required to facilitate the Olympics caused considerable concern to local residents as did the fact that the park would be unavailable for them to use for many months. However, although it took a year to restore the park to its former glory, no trees were lost and it was almost as if the Olympics never happened.

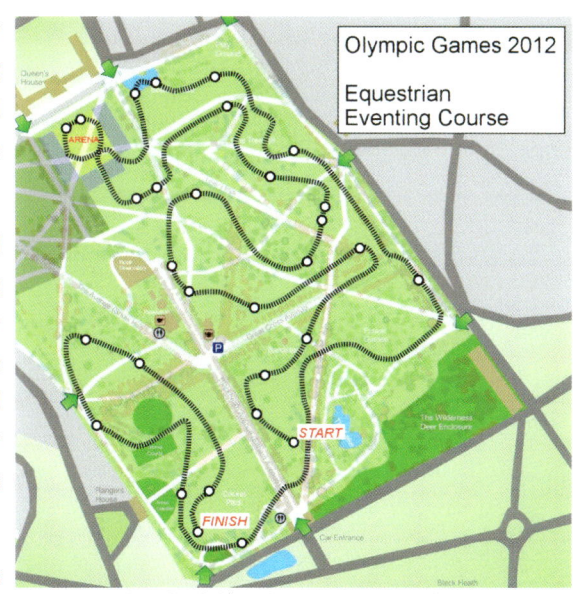

Image 211: 2012 Olympics equestrian eventing course.

Results Table

At the end of the Olympics Great Britain came third overall with 65 medals. Three of the golds came from Greenwich Park.

Event	Gold	Silver	Bronze
Individual Dressage	Great Britain	Netherlands	Great Britain
Team Dressage	Great Britain	Germany	Netherlands
Individual Eventing	Germany	Sweden	Germany
Team Eventing	Germany	Great Britain	New Zealand
Individual Jumping	Switzerland	Netherlands	Ireland
Team Jumping	Great Britain	Netherlands	Saudi Arabia

Greenwich Park Time Line

Year	Event
65m YA	Greenwich Park under a warm shallow sea.
c.8000 BC	Ice age ends, Thames moves south to flow past Greenwich Park.
c.4000 BC	Neolithic settlers occupy the area.
c.35	The Romans build Watling Street through the park and a Temple to Jupiter.
c.410	The Romans leave Britain and abandon the temple in the park.
c.600	Anglo Saxons inhabit the park and build a cemetery of burial barrows.
871	King Alfred recorded as owning Greenwich Park.
918	Greenwich Park given to the Abbey of St. Peter in Ghent.
1011	The Viking, Thorkell the Tall, sets up camp in Greenwich Park.
1012	Alfege, Archbishop of Canterbury, murdered in Greenwich.
1044	Edward the Confessor reaffirms the rights of the Abbey of St. Peter in Ghent to Greenwich and Lewisham
1071	The titles to Greenwich and Lewisham seized by the Flemish lord, Robert the Frisian.
1200	Queen Elizabeth's Oak begins growing.
1222	Greenwich and Lewisham returned to the Abbey of St. Peter in Ghent.
1286	First records of a Thames-side manor in Greenwich used by the Monks of Lewisham Priory, an Alien House for the Abbey of St. Peter in Ghent.
1300	Edward I visits Old Court in Greenwich to make an offering.
1337	Edward III starts the 100 years war against France and confiscates Greenwich Park from the abbey on the grounds of its strategic position and Ghent being allied with France.
1408	Henry IV visits Old Court.
1414	Old Court seized by Henry V on the dissolution of Alien Houses.
1426	Thomas Beaufort, Duke of Exeter, leases Old Court.
1433	Humphrey, Duke of Gloucester, inherits Old Court and begins building a new palace called Bella Court. He encloses the surrounding land with a fence, forming Greenwich Park.

1437	Greenwich Park is completely enclosed and a castle built on the highest point (where the observatory now is).
1447	Greenwich Park and Bella Court are taken by Margaret of Anjou, wife of Henry VI. She renames the palace 'Pleasuance'.
1450	Jack Cade marches on London as part of the Peasant's Revolt and camps on Blackheath.
1451	Henry VI forces the Kentish men of Greenwich to kneel before him on Blackheath just outside the gate to the park.
1461	Edward IV hunts in Greenwich Park.
1464	Edward IV gives Pleasaunce and Greenwich Park to his wife, Elizabeth Woodville.
1481	Edward IV founds the House of Observant Friars in Greenwich just to the west of the Palace.
1487	Henry VII 'forces' Elizabeth Woodville out of Pleasaunce and makes it his favourite palace.
1491	Henry VIII born in the palace at Greenwich and christened in St Alfege's Church.
1497	Cornish rebels march on London protesting at Henry VII taxing tin mines. They are defeated at the Battle of Deptford Bridge on Blackheath.
1499	Henry VII begins rebuilding Pleasuance and renames it the Palace of Placentia.
1509	Henry VIII inherits the Palace of Placentia on becoming king and makes it his home.
1510	Henry VIII restocks the park with deer.
1516	The future Queen Mary is born in Greenwich to Catherine of Aragon.
1519	Henry VIII and Anne Boleyn court in Greenwich Park and dance under the Old Oak (Queen Elizabeth's Oak).
1520	Henry VIII develops a huge sports complex including a new tiltyard between the Palace of Placentia and Greenwich Park.
1533	The future Queen Elizabeth I is born in Greenwich to Anne Boleyn.
1536	Henry VIII has a life-changing accident in the tiltyard at Greenwich. He can no longer take part in sports.
1540	Anne of Cleves is met on Blackheath and brought to the Palace of Placentia through the park.

1553	Mary becomes queen and reverts the House of the Observant Friars to Catholicism She largely ignores Greenwich.
1558	Elizabeth I becomes queen and immediately makes the Palace of Placentia her home, restoring the fortunes of Greenwich.
1579	Queen Elizabeth's lover, Robert Dudley is briefly imprisoned in Greenwich Castle for getting married.
1605	Henry Howard buys the rights to be Park Keeper and refurbishes and enlarges Greenwich Castle.
1614	James I replants some of the park and it is first described as a garden with poplar trees lining the avenues.
1615	Anne of Denmark, wife of James I, commissions the building of the Queen's House overlooking the park.
1619	James I begins building a brick wall around the park.
1635	The Queen's House is finally completed by Charles I for his wife Henrietta Maria.
1649	Soldiers are stationed in Greenwich Castle to protect the deer from poachers.
1653	Oliver Cromwell tries to sell the Queen's House and the park on behalf of the Commonwealth.
1654	Oliver Cromwell occupies the Queen's House, the sale having failed. The Palace of Placentia becomes a biscuit factory.
1660	Charles II demolishes the irreparable Palace of Placentia and builds part of a new palace. This now makes up the west wing of the Naval College.
1661	Sir William Boreman begins replanting and landscaping the park. This includes creating The Wilderness, planting chestnut and elm on the avenues and making the terrace and giant steps next to Greenwich Castle.
1662	Boreman's giant steps are admired by Samuel Pepys. Charles II invites the great landscape architect, André Le Nôtre, to Greenwich and receives some plans for a parterre from him.
1664	The landscaping of the parterre is completed.
1665	Charles II abandons the great landscaping of the park, ostensibly because there is not enough water to service the cascade and fountains he wants.
1676	The Royal Observatory is built to map the stars, replacing the crumbling Greenwich Castle.

Year	Event
1692	Mary and William III commission the building of a Naval Hospital incorporating the unused and half completed palace started by Charles II.
1697	The road running under the Queen's House is moved to its current location and named Romney Road.
1698	Standard House Reservoir is built by Nicholas Hawksmoor.
1703	The worst storm in history results in many trees on the upper ground being lost and some of the brick wall is brought down.
1705	The Naval Hospital opens.
1726	Voltaire visits Greenwich Park and describes a public fair taking place.
1743	Park Ranger, Lady Caroline Pelham, begins restoring the park.
1784	First excavations of the Anglo Saxon Tumuli.
1790	Neville Maskelyne builds a new path up to the observatory, partially filling in the terraces.
1800	A violent storm brings down many trees.
1806	The Queen's House becomes a school. Caroline of Brunswick, the Park Ranger, fences in five acres of the park as her Garden.
1808	St. Mary's Lodge is built as a gatehouse.
1809	Ha-ha built to replace the northern wall of the park.
1812	A Survey of the park reveals only 20 of the remaining 3000 trees are in good health.
1815	The popular Princess Sophia Matilda occupies the Ranger's House as Park Ranger.
1820	Greenwich Park is declared a public park by George IV.
1823	The foundation stone of St Mary's Church is laid. It is completed in 1824.
1825	Magistrates attempt to ban Greenwich Fair and prevent it taking place in the park.
1833	The red time-ball is added to the observatory.
1836	Charles Dickens describes Greenwich Fair in 'Sketches by Boz'.
1840	Work is undertaken on the slopes below the observatory to stabilise its foundations.
1846	Western Admiralty Reservoir is constructed.
1847	Altazimuth Pavilion is built.
1848	A storm blows down the one tree on One Tree Hill and it is replaced by the current London plane.

1852	The Shepherd Gate Clock is installed outside the observatory providing accurate time to the public.
1853	The Keeper's Cottage is demolished and the Keeper's Lodge at Blackheath gate built to replace it.
1854	The ornamental flower garden is laid-out, pioneering a new concept in public parks.
1855	The wooden gates at the Blackheath entrance are replaced with the modern wrought iron gates.
1857	Greenwich Fair permanently banned.
1860	The Great Equatorial Building of the observatory is erected but with a cylindrical roof.
1870	The Naval Hospital closes.
1873	The Naval College is founded and takes over the old Naval Hospital buildings.
1875	Horses, carriages and cyclists are allowed into the park from Blackheath.
1884	On October 13, the Greenwich meridian is formally adopted as the zero meridian for measuring longitude by all nations.
1887	Horses, carriages and cyclists are allowed to use the road through the park from Greenwich to Blackheath.
1891	Construction of the South Building at the observatory begins. The bandstand is installed.
1894	An anarchist detonates a bomb on the path up to the observatory. The last of the original Scots pine trees on the Charles II terraces is felled.
1897	An oak tree is planted to celebrate Queen Victoria's Jubilee.
1898	The American Garden and the Dell are planted with shrubs.
1902	The Grace and Favour position of Greenwich Park Ranger abolished.
1925	The ha-ha is partially filled-in and made into a herbaceous border.
1927	The deer are confined to The Wilderness and are no longer free to roam the park.
1929	The modern St. Mary's gate is installed.
1930	The statue of General Sir James Wolfe is unveiled. The boating lake is put in place.
1936	St. Mary's Church is demolished.
1937	The Strologo Bus Shelter is built.

1940	The area in front of The Queen's House is dug up for allotments and bomb shelters are built.
1946	The Royal Observatory closes and moves its operations to Herstmonceaux in Sussex.
1950	Blackheath Avenue is replanted with horse chestnuts and the cherry tree avenue planted.
1970	Dutch elm disease begins to kill the remaining elm trees.
1975	100 mature elms are felled due to Dutch elm disease leaving just a handful of elms remaining.
1977	An avenue of trees is planted in front of The Queen's House to celebrate Queen Elizabeth II's Silver Jubilee.
1979	The Henry Moore statue "Knife Edge" is installed (it was subsequently removed and replaced in 2012).
1987	A storm on the 16th October brings down almost 400 trees.
1990	Another great storm fells many trees including the dead, but still upright, Queen Elizabeth's Oak.
1992	A new oak is planted at the site of Queen Elizabeth's Oak by the Duke of Edinburgh destroying the last remaining remnant of the original hunting park vegetation in the park.
1994	A geophysical survey of the Anglo Saxon tumuli establishes their location and number.
1998	The Royal Observatory becomes part of the National Maritime Museum.
1999	The sundial by the boating lake is installed and avenues either side of the Parterre are enhanced for the new millennium.
2007	The planetarium opens at the observatory.
2012	Greenwich Park hosts the equestrian events for the London Olympics.
2013	The Queen's Orchard opens to the public.
2021	Significant work on improving the park begins, having been delayed by the Covid-19 crisis.

Index

Abbey of St Peter in Ghent....................19, 21 ff.
Acid grassland..9 f.
Air Raid Shelter..157
Airy, George..................................91, 103, 131
Alien House...19, 23
All Saints Church..70
Allotments..76, 222
Altazimuth Pavilion...................................92, 103
American Garden....................................125, 128
Anarchist Bomb...98
Anglo Saxons....................16, 19, 22 f., 26, 165
Anti-aircraft guns..76
Armada Portrait...135
Armoury...36
Astronomer Royal..80, 82, 91, 94, 100, 103, 131
Avenues.....................55, 58 f., 61, 64, 171 f., 186
Babington, Uriah...47
Bandstand...75, 147 f.
Bee wolf wasp...235
Beech Tree.........................170, 172, 186 f., 192
Bella Court..26 ff., 153
Birds...232
Blackheath......8, 29 f., 38, 59, 61, 70, 72 f., 111, 129, 140, 153
Blackheath Avenue..........70, 148, 172, 182, 196
Blackheath Formation...8
Blackheath Gate...............8, 38, 69, 73, 119, 128
Blossom...171, 196 f.
Boating lake..150 ff., 163
Boleyn, Anne..37, 200
Bombs...95
Boreman, William......................48, 57, 60 f., 64
Bourdin, Martial..98
Britannia..167
Burial Mounds..17, 165
Butterflies...234
Caroline of Brunswick...........................121, 125
Catherine of Aragon..............................32, 136
Chalk..4, 8, 30
Charles I..46 f., 120, 122
Charles II......46, 49 f., 57 ff., 80 ff., 120, 122, 166
Cherry Tree..196 f.
Chesterfield House...............................125, 130
Cleves, Anne of..38

Cobham, Eleanor...28
Common bent...10
Conduits. 23, 48, 59, 66, 102, 153, 155 f., 159 f., 162 f.
Cornish Rebel..72
Cromwell, Oliver......................................47, 118
Croom's Hill...........................27, 116, 131, 153
Cuckoo wasp..235
Cutty Sark...105
De Caus, Salomon......................................43, 55
Deer............32, 54 f., 79, 118, 216, 224 ff., 228 f.
Dell...8, 125, 128
Dickens, Charles...142
Doomsday Book...22
Dragonflies...234
Dudley, Robert..41, 79
East Greenwich Pleasaunce...........................169
East India Company...42
Ecosystem..9
Edward I..24
Edward III..24
Edward IV..30, 77
Edward the Confessor..................................22 f.
Edward V...31
Edward VI..38 f., 67
Elizabeth I.........................40, 79, 135 f., 200
Elm Tree...64, 172, 184, 198
Eltham...61, 102
Eltham Palace.....................................24, 69, 224
Ethelred (Æthelred)...................................19, 21
Evelyn, John..140
Flamstead House.........................80, 83 f., 89, 100
Flamstead, John.................................80, 82, 87
Flamstead's Well..84
Flower Garden. 64, 76, 103, 172, 202, 206, 214, 216, 231 f.
Foxes...230 f.
Gentileschi, Orazio..................................46, 134
George III..89, 125
George IV...125
Ginkgo tree...213
Great Cross Avenue.........................103, 148, 172
Great Equatorial Building................................92
Great Trees of London...................................202

244

Green-eyed flower bee...................................234
Greenwich Castle..38, 49, 60, 77 f., 84, 112, 117
Greenwich Fair......................68, 140, 142, 144 ff.
Grinling Gibbons..184
Gronewic..16, 19
Hanami..197
Harrison, John...87
Hawksmoor, Nicholas...............75, 155, 159, 162
Hawthorn Tree...210
Henrietta Maria..................................46, 57, 134
Henry Howard, Lord Northampton.........78, 117
Henry IV..24, 26
Henry V...24 ff.
Henry VI...................................25, 27, 29 f., 153
Henry VII..31 f., 72
Henry VIII...........31 ff., 36, 38, 78, 133, 136, 200
Herb Garden..220
Herbaceous Border..................................66, 222
Himalayan Cedar Tree...................................206
Holm Oak Tree...181
Hornbeam Tree..172
Horse Chestnut Tree...........................172, 182 f.
Hosier, Francis...129
Humphrey, Duke of Gloucester 26 f., 55, 77, 153
Hunting...32, 37, 54 f., 78, 224
Ice Age...5, 207
Ice House..101 f.
Isle of Dogs..6
Jack Cade..8, 29 f.
James I..43, 55, 101, 117
James II..121
Jones, Inigo..44, 133
Jousting...32, 37
Keeper's Cottage...................57, 118, 160 f., 200
Keeper's Lodge..69, 119
King Alfred..19, 22
Knife Edge..113 f.
Knollys, Lettice..41
Lake..203, 216
Landscaping......................54, 57, 61, 69, 208
Le Nôtre, André...58
Lesnes Abbey...55, 175
Lewisham Priory..19
Lime Tree............................113, 172, 184 f.
Limekiln..8
Loggia..133

London Clay..4
London Plane Tree.................108, 189, 191, 194
Macartney House......................................97, 130
Magnetic Observatory...................................103
Margaret of Anjou......................................27 ff.
Mary I..39
Mary of York...77
Maskelyne, Neville..83
Maze Hill............................27, 75, 162, 178
Meridian...........................85 ff., 92 ff., 151
Mining bee..234 f.
Mirefleur...77 f.
Mollet, André..55 f.
Montagu House.........................121 ff., 125 f.
Moore, Henry...113 f.
Moore, Jonas...80 ff.
National Maritime Museum................36, 69, 93
Naval College.........................52, 66, 105, 113
Naval Hospital......48 ff., 75, 112, 116, 121, 132,
 153, 157, 164, 169, 222
Normans...22 f.
Oak Tree............170, 172, 178, 180, 199 ff., 213
Observant Friars..........................31 f., 36 f., 39
Observatory...3, 11, 49, 53, 60, 77, 80 ff., 85, 89
 ff., 98, 100, 103, 105, 113, 130 f., 166, 169
Observatory Garden...........................8, 100 ff.
Old Court..............................23 f., 26, 117, 153
Olympic Games....................113, 133, 236 f.
One Tree Hill.8 f., 48, 108, 110 f., 162, 178, 186,
 189, 199
Our Ladye Star of the Sea Church.........113, 116
Palace of Placentia....31 ff., 36, 38 f., 49, 66, 132
Palladio...133
Park Keeper...17, 98, 117
Park Ranger..117, 120 f., 125
Park Vista..............................66 f., 116, 163
Parterre.................................58 f., 61, 76, 133
Pavilion Tea House..148
Pebble Beds..4, 8
Pelham, Catherine..............................120 f., 140
Pepys, Samuel...140
Planetarium...93, 103
Playground..152
Pleasaunce..29 ff., 163
Pole Hill..94
Princess Sophia Matilda..................................68

Pump..119, 160, 200
Queen Anne...43, 117
Queen Caroline's Bath..126
Queen Elizabeth's Bower...................................11, 178
Queen Elizabeth's Oak......57, 118 f., 160, 199 f., 213
Queen Mary..39, 50
Queen's House 32, 36, 44, 47, 50 f., 57 f., 60, 65 f., 76, 105, 120 f., 132 f., 141, 166, 169, 178, 222, 236 f.
Queen's Orchard..57, 222
Railway..104, 168 f.
Ranger's House..129 f., 218
Reservoirs.............17, 76, 153, 155 ff., 160 f., 164
Richard Plantagenet..30
Rockery...128
Roman Statue..12 f.
Roman Temple...11, 13 ff.
Romans..11 ff., 19, 27, 176
Rose and Crown..68, 141
Rose Garden...........................122, 186, 196, 218
Royal Parks...................................2, 53, 71, 222
Rustic Fountain...161
Sackville, Charles...120
Saint Alfege..20 f.
Samuel Pepys...58
Sancho, Ignatius..123
Sand...4, 8 f., 101, 108
Scots Pine Tree..207 f.
Sequoia (Red Wood) Tree......................................209
Shagbark Hickory Tree..203
Sheen Priory...24, 27
Sheep's sorrel..10
Snow Hill..102, 163, 184
Snow Well...101 f., 163
Soil..9
Sophia Matilda..130
Spanish Chestnut Tree...................172, 175, 202
Squirrels..230
St. Alfege's Church. 32, 48, 69, 97, 130, 163, 184
St. Mary's Church..69
St. Mary's Gate...70, 184, 189
St. Mary's Lodge..68

Stag beetle..234
Standard House...155 f.
Statues............68, 95, 105, 113, 130, 167
Stockwell...68, 102, 153
Strologo..71
Sundial...151
Sycamore Tree................................172, 191, 194 f.
Thames 3 ff., 11, 15, 24, 41 f., 48 f., 53, 78 f., 89, 105, 108, 129, 140
The Point...74
Thorkell the Tall..20 f.
Tilbury..83, 136
Tiltyard..32, 37, 163
Time Ball..3, 89 f.
Time Lady..91
Tradescant, John..43, 46, 191
Tulip Tree...212
Tumuli...17 f., 163
Underground................................76, 155 f., 161
Vanbrugh Castle...108, 111 f.
Vanbrugh Gate...................................8, 178, 202
Vanbrugh, John...111
Versailles..46, 58, 60, 166
Vicarage..161, 163
Victorians..116, 142, 144 f., 147
Vikings..19 ff.
Voltaire...140
Walls..............48, 55, 65, 69, 73 f., 122, 129, 163
War Memorial...74
Watling Street......................................11, 14 f., 19, 27
Wernher, Julius..130
White House..131
Wilderness...57, 64, 178, 182, 215, 224 f., 231 f.
William IV...68
William the Conqueror..22
Wolfe, General James.........................95, 97, 130
Woodville, Elizabeth...30 f.
Woolwich Road......................36, 65, 121, 132, 169
World War II...................................8, 95, 157, 222
Wren, Christopher........................50, 60, 81 ff.
Wyngaerde..77
Yuri Gagarin..93